Books by
WILLIAM TRUFANT FOSTER
AND
WADDILL CATCHINGS

———

MONEY

PROFITS

BUSINESS WITHOUT A BUYER

THE ROAD TO PLENTY

———

POLLAK FOUNDATION FOR ECONOMIC RESEARCH
NEWTON 58, MASSACHUSETTS, U. S. A.

PUBLICATIONS
OF THE POLLAK FOUNDATION FOR
ECONOMIC RESEARCH

NUMBER ELEVEN
THE ROAD TO PLENTY

THE ROAD TO PLENTY

BY

WILLIAM TRUFANT FOSTER

AND

WADDILL CATCHINGS

Authors of 'Money,' 'Profits,' and 'Business Without a Buyer'

BOSTON AND NEW YORK
HOUGHTON MIFFLIN COMPANY
The Riverside Press Cambridge
1928

XR14
F75R6

The Riverside Press
CAMBRIDGE · MASSACHUSETTS
PRINTED IN THE U.S.A.

STAGES OF THE JOURNEY

THE ROAD TO PLENTY

THE ROAD TO PLENTY

. .

SECTION I

IN WHICH THE GRAY MAN AND THE THREE WISE MEN SHOW WHAT IT IS ALL ABOUT

A STOUT and florid manufacturer in a pink silk shirt, sitting next to the window in the smoking-room of a west-bound train out of Boston, pointed with a jerk of his thumb to a group of men in overalls, just outside a railroad repair shop. 'Trouble with those fellers is, never know when they're well off,' he growled. 'No matter how much you pay 'em, always want more.'

The speaker was a self-made man — very successfully made. No need for him to tell you so; though you had a feeling that he was sure to tell you, nevertheless.

Next to him sat a bond salesman, latest model. 'Commander,' 'Supreme Six,' 'Champion' — any one of the latest names would do. In his brand-new derby hat and his self-conscious necktie, he seemed to have burst forth at that moment from an advertisement in the ponderous magazine which he held in his hand. He had recently been graduated from 'the very best college in the country' — a large college, he said, but there are those who love it — and the truth had forced itself upon him that he knew a great deal. That, too, you could see for yourself; though, again, you had an uneasy feeling that you would have to hear it all, sooner or later, from his own lips.

'If they're not satisfied with what they're gettin',' snapped the Self-Made Man, 'let 'em work the way I did. Plenty of chance. Any one who don't succeed like I have, it's his own fault. Already gettin' more wages than they got sense enough to spend; yet always shoutin' for more.'

'Quite so,' chimed in the Bond Salesman, well pleased with himself for agreeing with an illiterate manufacturer of stove polish. The very best college in the country was proud of its democracy. 'Well, here we are at Linton.'

The train slowed down as it passed a row of sooty mills and a row of sootier tenements. Sootiest of all were the workers, assembled at the station where the train stopped. A group of them — mill hands, out of work — were saying good-bye to a slender little gray-haired man, in a gray suit and a gray felt hat, with a smile in radiant contrast to all his grayness. One of the workers, the stalwart one with a ragged scar on his pale forehead, seemed especially loath to let the Gray Man go; held him, in fact, by both arms, looking down into his face as the Gray Man spoke earnestly. He was talking, it seemed, in a last effort to put courage into the heart of his broad-shouldered friend. And well might he try, for the down-and-out condition of the man's clothes was more than matched by the down-and-out cast of his countenance.

Through the open window of the smoking-room, the travelers heard the Gray Man say: 'Keep a stiff upper lip, Joe. There must be something we can do. We'll try again, as soon as I get back from Chicago.'

A clanging of bells and a last rush of passengers.

Meantime, another man had taken a seat in the smoking-room, removed a document from his green bag, and lighted a cigar. He had a kind face and a strong one, and you felt sure that whatever he said would come from a good heart. He was reserved and self-assured in manner, subdued and nondescript in dress, correct and formal in speech. Any one might have inferred, without going far wrong, that the newcomer was an attorney-at-law, Boston-born and Boston-bred, a life-long Republican, a bank director, and a regular reader of the *Transcript*. And, naturally, he was a graduate of Harvard College. He was not really 'as solitary and self-contained as an oyster,' though doubtless the other men thought he was.

The train started with a jerk and rumbled along. So did the Self-Made Man. 'Workers gettin' on as well as any one could expect, I'll say. No more than the usual amount of unemployment.'

The Little Gray Man heard those remarks just as he came into the smoking-room — heard them and shrugged his shoulders. Relaxed he was now, and sad. Evidently his cheerful good-byes to the mill hands had been more than half acting.

'The working classes were never so well off,' agreed the Bond Salesman. 'Statistics prove conclusively that since 1914, real wages have increased twenty per cent. Deposits in savings banks have doubled. Poverty is virtually abolished.'

The Brakeman, who was washing his hands in the corner, looked over his shoulder at the speaker; but he could not flag that train of thought with a look; so the Bond Salesman ran on.

'Ours is the most prosperous country on earth,' he

declared. 'Statistics for pig-iron production tell the story. But you don't need statistics. Look at the automobiles, lined up at every little soap-box of a station. Look at the electric lights, washing machines, radios, motion pictures. Look at the clothes the workers buy. Why, no self-respecting shop girl would be seen on the streets without silk stockings and a fur coat.'

'Right you are,' nodded the Self-Made Man. 'Didn't have them luxuries when I was a boy. And work? Say, I worked twelve hours a day, Saturdays included. Three dollars a week. Nowadays people don't know what work is. That's the trouble with 'em.'

While this ultimatum was being delivered, a big man, in a big felt hat, took the big armchair and lighted a big cigar. A Dirt Farmer from the Wide West, that was certain, and dressed for the part; the very man to give a touch of reality to the Great Open Spaces of Hollywood.

Then the democratic Bond Salesman, deftly withdrawing from a silver case a monogrammed cigarette, and tapping it on his magazine, continued his remarks: 'What would they do with more money, if they had it?' he asked; and at once he answered his question with that finality which comes from experience — if it is not too extensive. 'Merely squander it, imitating the heroes and heroines in the movies, trying to live above their station in life, paying a dollar down here and a dollar down there, mortgaging wages which they may never get, and piling up ——'

'That's it,' interrupted the Self-Made Man. 'Tryin' to get somethin' for nothin'. How can they expect to get what they don't earn? Where's it comin' from?

That's what I'd like to know. Can't pay 'em wages except out of what they make. If they want more, let 'em get busy an' produce more.'

The Gray Man smiled — faintly. He thought of his friend Joe Burns, the dejected man with the ragged scar on his pale forehead, who had clung to him on the station platform. As the Gray Man understood it, Joe Burns was without work, and a million other men throughout the country — coal miners, shoe makers, farm laborers, even automobile mechanics, as well as mill hands — were out of jobs at that very moment because they had produced too much, more than could be sold. He thought of asking the Self-Made Man how these workers could have improved their lot by turning out still more goods.

But the Bishop began to preach — the complacent, pompous, round-faced, well-kept Bishop, sitting in the corner, who had been getting ready all this time, as the Gray Man knew from sad experience, to make the pronouncement that all economic problems are fundamentally moral.

'The root of the trouble is that the people are worshiping false gods,' declared the Bishop, folding his hands across his ample waist. 'They want more money, more money, always more money, while true happiness is found only in spiritual wealth. What would they do with more money? Most of them already have the necessities and a lot of the questionable luxuries of life. With more money they would buy more face powder, no doubt, more perfumes and jewelry, more immodest gowns, more radio sets, more cigarettes, more ——'

'Yes,' snorted the Self-Made Man, 'and take more joy-rides and work less.'

'Already,' placidly continued the Bishop, twirling his thumbs, 'our dear people have lost some of the sturdy qualities of their hard-working forefathers. As wealth accumulates, men decay. My friends, you cannot worship both God and Mammon.'

'You said it, Bishop,' responded the Self-Made Man. 'People too darn prosperous; life too easy. That's what's the matter.'

Under the big felt hat was an expression of amazement; for the Farmer had discovered, without the help of the *Congressional Record*, that the country has a farm problem; and he was about to remark that out where he lived, ten hours a day of hard work didn't guarantee any family the necessities of life, to say nothing of joy-rides. He would like to tell the Bishop that no farmer, or farmer's wife, or farmer's daughter, whom he had happened to meet in all the wide stretches of the Wide West, was destroying moral fiber with luxurious living.

But the Bond Salesman went on dispensing information: 'There is no use blaming the mill owners for shutting down. What else can they do? If half the looms ran full time every week in the year, more cloth would be produced than the whole country could buy.'

'Then why in the name of common sense,' cried the Self-Made Man, 'don't the surplus men go to work somewhere else?'

'In your own factory?' suggested the Gray Man, gently, endeavoring to bring into the conversation at least a touch of the realities of life.

'Well, not now,' answered the Self-Made Man, making an unsuccessful effort to throw his cigar butt into the cuspidor across the room. 'Fact is, I'm lettin' off a lot of men. Just put in new machines; keep my factory right up to the minute; don't need half as many men as I useter.'

'Nothing uncommon about that,' remarked the Lawyer, looking up from the document which he held in his hands. 'It is going on all over the world. A serious problem in Germany, the Agent-General for Reparations says, is the large increase in the unemployed, caused by the adoption of various methods for the better utilization of labor.'

'Just so,' observed the Gray Man in his quiet voice. 'Where, I wonder, can our own "surplus" men find work? Not on that big construction job we just passed. "No MEN WANTED"; and you have seen signs like that everywhere. This country may be too prosperous, but the three million workers without steady jobs don't believe it, nor the many million more who don't know for sure whether their jobs will last another week. Anyway, our prosperity seems nothing to boast about when the people who suffer from want are more numerous than those who have all that is good for them.'

'For this materialistic country,' intoned the Bishop, impervious to all that the Gray Man had said, 'there is only one way to salvation. Some great calamity must save us from the flesh-pots of Egypt. I tell you, my friends, we must pass through cleansing fires of renunciation, as have our brethren in Europe. We, too, must suffer — suffer.'

At that point the Little Gray Man, sure that staying

any longer with the Three Wise Men of the East would mean nothing but suffering for him, escaped from the overheated discussion and the overheated room.

Suffer! The Gray Man wished that, once in a while, he could forget what he knew about suffering. But he never could put out of mind the plight of the unemployed, as he saw it every day. Nor could he ever quite lose his poignant memories of the winter, years before, when he himself had suffered from 'hard times.'

Always there loomed before him the menacing specter of another big slump; for everywhere he went, he found men talking about the next depression as though it were foreordained, like the movements of the moon. Yet, apparently, nothing could induce these men to wrestle with the problem before the worst had happened; and then it was too late. Like the shiftless farmer, thought the Little Gray Man, who never got his leaky roof repaired, because he saw no need of mending it in fair weather, and could not mend it in rainy weather.

For a while the Little Gray Man stood on the car platform. Through the door he saw house after house that told the story of anything but luxury; house after house without even a lawn or a visible coat of paint. Then he thought of the farms he had seen in all parts of the country, most of which had not achieved the luxury of tractors, or telephones, or electric lights, or running water, to say nothing of comfortable heating and plumbing. He thought, too, of the feeble grandparents he had seen, struggling with work beyond their strength; and he recalled the fact that right there in Massachusetts, one of the wealthiest communities in the world, more than half the aged are unable to support themselves, out of either wages or savings. Indeed, the Gray Man knew perfectly well, for he was engaged in poor relief, that even in Massachusetts a fourth of the old people are making hopeless efforts to live decently and comfortably on less than four hundred dollars a year and such meager aid as they get from relatives and charity.

Then he thought of those cocksure men in the smoking-room, spending freely for their own comfort and freely judging the spending of others. With what fortitude they endure the privations of other people! 'Oh, well,' he said to himself, 'they are ignorant, both the educated and the uneducated; equally ignorant. The Bond Salesman's education is too much for his intelligence; the Self-Made Man's success is too much for his. And that protected Bishop! He, of all the Wise Men, is most out of touch with the real world.'

The Gray Man felt sure that those men would change their views, if they lived even a single day with Joe Burns and his wife and two children in the row of tenements next to the freight yards.

Joe had worked in the mill until work had stopped; stopped because it had been done too well; stopped because the mills had produced too much cloth; cloth that piled up in the warehouses, while orders fell off.

Then, week after week, Joe had hunted for a job. Every morning he had started out with a little hope; every day he had dragged himself from one disappointment to another; every night he had returned, empty-handed, hope gone, to face the eyes of wife and children.

In those first dark days, they had asked the question — the one question on which their health, their sense of decency, everything, seemed to hang. But they had long since given up asking. Before he entered the room they read the answer in the heavy step of the defeated man.

A month of this; a month during which he spent all that was left of his savings, all that he had managed to put aside by cutting down on milk and meat and by renting one of his four rooms to a stranger. Then one day, after he had found a job shoveling snow off a roof, he slipped and got that gash in his head.

After that came the fever which kept him in bed for a month; a month without money for hospital care, without money even for home care; a month dependent on the pittance which is the utmost that charity can afford.

Was it all Joe's fault? No doubt the uneducated man in the pink silk shirt would say so; no doubt the educated man in the new derby hat would say so. Yet how could any one put all the blame on Joe? He had worked faithfully, as long as he had work to do. Everybody knew that. He did nobody any wrong, bore nobody ill-will; for he had not yet become embittered by blasted hopes. He was contented as long as the early-morning whistle blew for him. As with most workers, so with Joe, his whole life revolved around his job. Without a job he could not carry his own weight. All he asked was a chance to work. And suddenly — for the life of him, he could not tell why — he was not allowed to work at all.

Job gone — savings gone — self-respect going — how long could he keep his home?

And such a home! The Gray Man shuddered. Where were the luxuries so glibly handed out to the poor, in the imaginations of the rich? Where, indeed, were the necessities? Not here, at least. Here poverty cried out to High Heaven for all that makes childhood romantic and gay. This flimsy tenement house, in the long row of tenement houses, all exactly alike, except that each seemed dirtier than the rest; this shapeless shack with its three families, its extra lodgers, its cracked walls, its foul odors, its ugly surroundings, its repulsive outhouses — was it in such dwellings that laborers squandered their excess wages?

How, in such a place — he would like to ask the Bishop — could human beings, with all their frailty and their yearnings, cultivate the things of the spirit? Could the Bishop expect men to be virtuous and contented here, with no hope of happiness except in the life to come? The Bishop, no doubt, felt the need of a happy life here and now, a life freed from its chief anxiety, a life in which a day's work was sure to yield, year in and year out, at least a decent living. Without that assurance, the Gray Man wondered, how much would most of us have left of what we call morals?

But the Bishop had said, 'What this country needs is to suffer — suffer.'

Suffer! The Gray Man could not hear the word without thinking of little Mary Marden, as he had seen her that morning, lying in the dingy sick-room, friendless, penniless. The plight of the Burnses was bad enough, but poor little Mary ——

The Brakeman stepped on to the platform. 'How is it with you?' asked the Gray Man, for he had noticed the Brakeman in the smoking-room. 'Could you spend an extra five dollars a week without losing your immortal soul?'

'Could I! Well, I might manage it. At least, I could begin paying off the mortgage on the house. But no,' he added, laying down his flags, 'I couldn't do that, either. There's Mother and the two kids to take care of; and Mother's eyes are too weak to take in sewing any longer, though she doesn't see how she can stop. You know how it is.'

The Gray Man certainly did know. He knew because, like twenty million other wage-earners, he had tried to take care of wife and children on no more than nineteen hundred dollars a year. He had found out, in the only way that any one ever does find out, just how luxuriously a family can live on such an income; how little can be saved; how long it takes the family fortunes to recover from the birth of a child; what a financial calamity a surgical operation can be.

He knew, too, how miserably others fare on such wages, even in what the fortunate call 'good times'; for his own work kept him in close touch with workers everywhere. The Brakeman was no exception; neither was Joe Burns. The exception, as the Gray Man knew perfectly well, was the head of a family who did *not* have some crushing anxiety that could be relieved by an extra five dollars a week.

The Bishop, it seemed, lived in another world — a world which knew little about the five million wage-earners who have no higher wages than Joe Burns, no higher hopes, no more days of certain employment, no more savings, no more resources when sickness strikes them down. But surely the Bishop did know that sickness comes, sooner or later, to all families — sickness with its worry, its loss of wages, its inroads on savings and on courage. Did the Bishop have any idea how many million women, as faithful as the mother of the little Burnses, as self-effacing and uncomplaining, had forced themselves through the weary round, year after year, hoping against hope, until hope was quite, quite gone? Would the Bishop say to them, 'What this country needs is to suffer — suffer'?

SECTION II

AT the next city the Three Wise Men left the train.

'There they go,' said the Little Gray Man, as he paced the floor, talking to the Farmer and the Lawyer. 'There they go with their stout leather bags and their stout leather convictions. A cab to the leading hotel, a hearty dinner, a look around the lobby, and they will report that the city is highly prosperous, and nobody suffering except those who refuse to work. What can you do with men like that? Meantime the employment agencies in this city are crowded with job-seekers, and thousands of families are close to the danger line. The death-rate among their children is only one proof of it.'

'Yet to hear those boobs talk,' exclaimed the Farmer, bringing down his fist on the arm of the chair, 'you'd think everybody in this country was sufferin' from fatty degeneration of the pocketbook. Fact is, there ain't one farmer in five who can pay himself a thousand dollars a year for his own labor; ain't one in five, either, who knows how he's ever goin' to pay off his mortgage. Most of 'em aren't earnin' two per cent on their capital.'

'Go to it!' cried the Gray Man, sitting down beside the Farmer. 'We both need to let off steam. Think of the United States, the wealthiest country in the *world*, not even paying its postal clerks nineteen hundred dollars a year. Think of the families I visited last winter for the Family Society of Philadelphia. Half of them either had no bathtub at all, or shared one with other families. Two thirds had less than fifteen hundred dollars a year, while two thousand is the lowest budget that *anybody* has figured for a workman's family of five. And even two thousand, as I know from experience, provides nothing for savings, insurance, recreation, nothing whatever for luxuries — unless,' he added after a pause, 'having a toilet is a luxury.'

'I don't know much about city folks,' said the Farmer, 'but most farmers would think *they* were in luxury if they had two thousand dollars a year, would think they were in Heaven, I reckon, for they never expect that much on earth. And talk about modern conveniences! Do you realize that four out of five farmhouses have no bathtubs, nine out of ten no runnin' water, or electric lights, or motor trucks?'

'But those Three Wise Men of the East,' exclaimed the Gray Man, coming down hard on his chief words, with a gesture of the right hand for each word, as though he were underlining it, 'those men seem to think that people are poor because they *like* poverty, keep their children away from dentists because they *prefer* aching teeth, wear dirty clothes because they *hate* clean ones. Gr-e-a-t Jupiter!'

'You didn't hear the worst, either,' the Farmer added. 'This mornin', before you got aboard, they tore on about our great prosperity. You can't learn those smug idiots anything. Tell 'em that more than half the counties in the West haven't a single hospital, and they say, " Well, they have radios, haven't they?" Tell 'em that half the farmers won't break even on this season's crops, an' they say, "Well, what about all the automobiles?" After I talk with such men an hour, I feel as if I'd been splittin' hard wood all day.'

'I suppose,' reflected the Gray Man, 'that farmers are like our own mill hands. If they could only be freed from worry, if they could only be sure of the plain necessities, they would gladly give up most of the modern conveniences. All my poor friend Joe Burns yearns for, mind you — his idea of Heaven on earth — is a steady job, with gradual increases of pay.'

The Kindly Lawyer, who had said nothing all this time, now turned to the Gray Man. 'I know how you feel,' he said, carefully putting his document back in the green bag. 'I feel much the same way. Still, you must admit that prosperity confronts you everywhere. Wages really are higher than ever before. The more things cost, the larger the demand. Trains crowded, beauty parlors crowded, colleges crowded, hotels crowded. Theater prices higher than ever, and the theaters crowded; a million dollars a week spent for theater tickets in New York City alone. I am told that the residents of Park Avenue, above Thirty-Fourth Street, spend one hundred million dollars a year on amusements, automobiles, candy, perfumes, jewelry, yachts, and women's clothes.'

'But all that,' objected the Gray Man, 'is small comfort to those who are left out. Comfort, did I say? More unhappiness rather. The cold fact is that the life you describe, which looms so large in reports of our astounding prosperity, is absolutely out of the question for most people. All they know about abundance is what they see in the papers or in the movies.'

Just then a man came into the smoking-room whom the Lawyer greeted with evident pleasure and respect. He was a professor of economics who had represented the United States, unofficially, in a number of European conferences. The Professor took the seat by the window. At once he filled his brier pipe and lighted it, wiped his horn-rimmed spectacles, put them on, and was preparing to read the book which he carried under his arm, when the Lawyer sat down beside him, saying, 'You should have come sooner, Professor; you might have learned something about economics. We were just wondering, as you came in, how far-reaching this prosperity really is that we read so much about, and that is so blatantly thrust in our faces, at least in New York City.'

'No complaint among teachers that it is excessive, I assure you,' said the Professor; 'but then, teachers, as you know, are an uncomplaining lot — pledged, like the monks of the Middle Ages, to poverty, celibacy, and obedience.'

At that point, the conversation was interrupted by the demand for tickets. The conductor, turning to a tall man who had just entered the room and taken the seat in the corner, said, 'I now have a drawing-room for you — Room A, in the car ahead.'

'Here is another traveler with superabundance,' said the Gray Man to himself. 'He probably thinks, if he thinks about it at all, that some people sit up all night in day coaches because they *prefer* to travel that way.'

But when the Gray Man turned and looked at the newcomer, he recognized him as a leading citizen of the Commonwealth; a director of the Federal Reserve Bank; a benefactor whose generosity was well known to the inner circle of social workers; the leader to whom every one had turned, with a common impulse, in Liberty Loan and Red Cross drives. First of all, however, he was a business man, a business man of wide and successful experience. A self-made man — very much so — but *this* one did not worship his creator.

'However prosperous we are,' remarked the Lawyer, as the conductor left the room, 'nobody knows when the next depression may occur. That is always a sobering thought to me. I shall never forget — it keeps coming back like a bad dream — the time when my father had to have a police guard, to and from his mill, to protect him from the men who dogged his steps and blocked his way. Not that they had any idea of assaulting him; they were merely begging for a chance to do the hardest kind of labor at twenty cents an hour.'

'I remember that,' said the Professor. 'It was in the depression of 1907.'

'Remember 1907! I ought to remember it, if anybody does!' exclaimed the Gray Man.

'Later on,' continued the Lawyer, 'I came closer to the struggles of the poor, close enough to have my eyes really opened. All my life I had read about average wages, cost of food, rising rents, medical expenses, unemployment — no end of statistics; but they meant scarcely anything to me.'

'No more than they mean to that young college dude, just sent forth to fill the world's cryin' need for information and bonds,' commented the Farmer.

'Exactly,' said the Kindly Lawyer. 'Statistics were nothing to me but columns of figures. I was like a child who thinks that every child has a nursemaid. But I have learned something. At one time I dealt with a thousand men who had not seen a pay envelope for six months.'

'Then,' said the Gray Man, 'you have had every opportunity to find out what it means to live in anxiety. Every opportunity,' he added, after a pause, 'except the one that counts most. I judge that you have never had the very common and wholly unappreciated opportunity of trying it yourself. I have.

'First imagine,' he continued, 'bringing up a family on five thousand dollars a year. That puts you among, say, the upper five million of the well-to-do. You can, if you wish, look down with complacence on the comparative poverty of a hundred million below you. Instead, you look up. You think how comfortable you would be if you had a little larger income, say a third more. You know how greatly that would add to your feeling of security. You could make your insurance nearer your needs; renovate the house; even do the planting that you have long wanted to do. At last, you could take the whole family to the seashore, without having your vacation spoiled by the guilty feeling that you should have put the money in the bank. Well, that is just how I once felt. Then, instead of realizing my ambition, I lost everything. I had to get along on two thousand dollars a year; a little more than the average wage, to be sure, but not half what my family had been living on.'

'Is it a fact,' asked the Lawyer incredulously, 'that the average wage is no more than that?'

'He is right,' answered the Professor. 'The average annual wage of industrial workers — including those who usually are left out of the statistics — is no more than nineteen hundred dollars; an amount which ——'

'And farm workers don't even get that,' broke in the Farmer.

'Unhappily that is true,' the Professor said earnestly; 'and a bad thing it is for all of us.'

'Which means,' continued the Gray Man, 'that most fathers are trying to support families on about five dollars a day. Now, then, suppose that you, yourself, are bringing up a family on five thousand dollars, as I was, and buckle down to the task of imagining just what it would mean to cut your expenses to two thousand. Give up your house and move into a small flat, cut your food bills in half, have your wife do three times as much hard work, stop your daughter's music lessons, decide what you will deny yourselves in order to provide your children with all the milk they ought to have. Figure out what your family would have left, and you will begin to see how hard-pressed most wage-earners are, even in these so-called prosperous days. You will find that nineteen hundred dollars *barely* covers the needs of a family for food, clothing, shelter, and ordinary sickness; it leaves *nothing* for extraordinary hard luck, *nothing* for vacations, insurance, travel, education, or old age. If you can imagine what that means, you will know how to answer the man who says, "The workers are mighty well off right now. Why not let well enough alone?"'

'You are certainly a Thorn in the Flesh,' said the Kindly Lawyer. 'The worst of it is, you are right. If we could produce more and get it into the hands of the people who need it most, there would be gains in comfort, health, good will — gains as well in refined pleasures, even in the things of the spirit, which the learned Bishop appears to be concerned about.'

'But,' protested the Professor, 'we *are* making gains in volume of production.'

'What prevents us from making greater gains?' asked the Gray Man. '*That* is what I can't see. Every day we read of new inventions and new sources of power that increase the productivity of labor ten-fold, twenty-fold, even fifty-fold. That high-power line there along the track tells the story. By the mere turning of a switch, we now command a *hundred* times more energy than all the man-power and all the horse-power of our grand-fathers' time. What science has done for industry is as marvelous as the Magic Lamp.'

'True,' said the Kindly Lawyer, 'the story is thrilling, the progress is almost incredible.'

'Yet for my friend, Joe Burns — the unemployed mill hand whom you said you noticed clinging to me on the station platform — for poor Joe Burns **and** millions in like plight, our marvelous progress *still* spells poverty. And this in spite of the hopes that have sprung so high, generation after generation. Think of it! The overthrow of despots, the abolition of slavery, the birth of free nations, the industrial revolution, the organization of labor, universal suffrage — hope after hope that has always left the promised plenty and security receding before the laborer like a mirage. Why, in spite of all this progress, is it still nothing but a hope?'

As he asked that question, the Gray Man looked expectantly toward the tall man in the corner, the one among his hearers who seemed to be following him most intently. But the Business Man still remained silent.

'The comfortable ones assure us,' continued the Gray Man, 'that there is nothing to worry about; "only the usual amount of unemployment." Like O. Henry's story of the railroad wreck. "The accident was not serious," the newspaper said. "Only the engineer was killed."'

'You do not need to convince *me* that we ought to prevent unemployment and poverty, as far as possible,' replied the Lawyer. 'But I cannot see how we can do much more than we are now doing; and it is foolish to allow ourselves to get distressed over what we cannot prevent. I find much comfort in that thought. Every day the morning paper reports enough suffering to unfit me for the day's work, if I took it all to heart. What is the use? There is very little we can do about it.'

'Why not?' remonstrated the Gray Man. 'That is just what *I* have never been able to understand. This country is already equipped to lift the standard of living of the workers. Those idle looms at Linton are nothing remarkable. There is unused capacity in *every* industry you can think of. Isn't that so?'

'It certainly is,' the Kindly Lawyer replied. 'Nearly every business man I know is afraid to run his business at any approach to capacity, but he is not to blame for being cautious.'

'Afraid of *over*production,' said the Gray Man, 'while many of the people who work for him are suffering from *under*consumption.'

'That seems to sum it up.'

'But it doesn't make sense. Time and again, it has driven me to the verge of socialism and various other "isms." It seems dreadful to sit by and do nothing. Joe Burns, who needs shoes for his children, is eager to make woolen cloth. His brother Andrew, who needs clothes for *his* children, is eager to make shoes. And neither man is allowed to work. Meantime, our friend the Farmer here, who wants not only cloth and shoes, but nearly everything else that we make in New England, cannot buy what *he* wants because he has produced too much of what *we* want. What is the sense of that?'

'No sense at all!' cried the Farmer.

'But there is another side to the picture,' protested the Kindly Lawyer. 'All of us would be worse off if we blew up the whole economic system. There is no use trying dynamite; the Russian experiment is not encouraging. After all, we are making progress.'

'Yes — a little progress,' admitted the Gray Man. 'I suppose the young Salesman is right about that, in spite of his college education.'

'Mighty little progress that we can see out where I live,' said the Farmer.

'But we could not do even as well as we have done,' the Lawyer asserted, 'without competition, rewards for individual effort, private property, profits ——'

'Inducements to work and save,' broke in the Professor.

'Yes; that is precisely what makes us produce so much now. And no system can give us more than we produce. The best we can do is to see that business has abundant credit. Then production will increase because everybody is seeking profits; production itself will furnish consumers the means of purchase; and so standards of living will be raised as they have been in the past. Adam Smith was right about that, as he was about most fundamentals; the "Invisible Hand" is still guiding us. The best we can do is to leave economic laws alone to work out our problems.'

'Yes,' said the Gray Man doubtfully, 'that is what you men who ought to know always tell me.'

'And that's what they're always tellin' us,' said the Farmer.

'And are we not right, Professor?' asked the Lawyer.

'In the main, yes, with some obvious qualifications,' answered the Professor. 'Socialists, communists, and most of the other radicals propose to do away with the chief incentives to productive effort, without providing any effective substitute. Or else they want to increase the volume of money artificially, not understanding that inflation makes matters worse. Most proposals for reform are made by men who think they have discovered something new, merely because they are not acquainted with technical literature. It would not take much research to disclose the fact that most of their proposals have been fully explored and discredited by economists.'

'Well, if that is so,' said the Gray Man sadly, 'most people have little to hope for. I wonder if you men know what a tragedy it is to condemn millions of people to such a dismal future.'

'Facts are facts, no matter how you may feel about the consequences,' replied the Lawyer. 'The business cycle follows natural laws. I have heard you explain all that, have I not, Professor?'

'I trust I did not use the phrase "natural laws." Few economists believe in a self-generating psychological rhythm. They do hold, however, that psychological factors intensify both boom and depression — operating, one might say, in a cumulative manner. Just as there is summer and winter, flood and drought, so there is undue optimism and overdevelopment of capital, followed by undue pessimism and shutting-down of factories. These extreme alternations of prosperity and depression are well grounded in human nature. We cannot prevent them.'

'That is the trouble,' agreed the Lawyer. 'At times business men are too grasping and produce without thought of the consequences. At other times, they have no courage and close down their plants. They are like a flock of sheep. Besides, they are always misjudging their markets and bringing on an unbalanced condition of industry. What we need chiefly is balanced production — the right volume of oil, textiles, shoes, and so on, in relation to the volume of other goods. Am I not right, Professor?'

'Yes, largely; and there is not much that we can do to get balanced production beyond keeping business men informed of stocks on hand and market conditions. There is no doubt you are right; meddling with human nature and economic laws always makes matters worse.'

'That may be true, for all I know,' said the Gray Man, wearily. 'I don't pretend to know what *can* be done about it. But as to whether anything *needs* to be done!

Ye gods! Can any one seriously question that? Perhaps *you* can comfort yourself with the gains we have made in well-being, but I can't. If a doctor tells me that there is no known cure for cancer, and so my mother *must* die, I don't know enough to argue with him. But if he tells me that, after all, there is nothing very bad about cancer — Gr-e-a-t Jupiter!'

Just then, as the train was drawing into a station, the place at which the Farmer evidently intended to leave, the green curtain was pushed aside and a shining black face appeared.

'First call for luncheon; dinin'-car in the rear.'

'Here's another economic problem,' said the Professor, starting for the door. 'But before we try to solve it, why not take advantage of this ten-minute stop and get a breath of fresh air?'

The Gray Man and the Lawyer followed the Professor out onto the platform, leaving the Business Man alone.

SECTION III

IN WHICH THE BUSINESS MAN THINKS AND THE
RED-HAIRED ORATOR ORATES

LEFT alone in the smoking-room, the Business Man lighted another cigar and thought it all over. He had to admit that he was moved by the divine unrest of the Little Gray Man, truly the Servant in the House. It was a fine and natural impulse which urged this comrade of the poor to hunt for a way out; to refuse to accept things as they are, when he was sure that things as they *might* be would prevent so much privation and anxiety. Such a generous impulse surely ought not to be suppressed. And so the Business Man was sorry that the Lawyer and the Professor had thrown cold water on the Gray Man's fires.

'That Lawyer has a kind heart,' said the Business Man to himself. 'So has the Professor; you can see that. No doubt they are as eager as the Little Gray Man to improve the lot of the workers. But what can they suggest to him? More charity, perhaps, when he is tired of handing out charity. He sees the need of something which will go to the root of enforced idleness and poverty. And they tell him there isn't anything.'

Yet the Business Man knew that it is precisely such men as the Lawyer and the Professor who must do something, if anything is to be done. They are the ones who have the brains to find the way and the power to command a following.

If only they had the anxiety of Joe Burns to spur

them on! But such men, fairly comfortable with the world as it is, are not impelled to wrestle with the problem. Meanwhile, those who suffer have plenty of impulse, but little knowledge. Unable to find out what the trouble is or where hope lies, they look toward one futile remedy after another.

'And there you are!' said the Business Man, still talking to himself. 'Those who have the urge, lack knowledge and power; those who have knowledge and power, lack the urge.'

The Business Man felt sure that the Lawyer and the Professor had acquired their ideas, at least in part, from generations which knew nothing of the industrial and financial world of to-day. Those ideas, moreover, had been built into a system of economics by men who did not understand exactly what was going on even at their own time, in the banks and the market places. Thus certain theories, originated long ago in the quiet of professors' studies, had been accepted by some professors with little attempt to bring them to the test of the highly developed, complicated, work-a-day world.

'So these men insist,' mused the Business Man, 'that there is not much we can do about it. Too bad that at all times millions have to be out of work; that every now and then more millions have to be thrown out; but it can't be helped. Too bad that we can't use half our productive powers, but of course we can't. Human nature blocks the way. No use trying to repeal economic laws. Slow and halting progress is all we can expect for the great masses of laborers. The fault is in the stars.

'Bunk!' he exclaimed aloud.

Relieved to that extent, he went on talking to himself. 'The venerable and respected Economics of Despair, at bottom little more than I was taught at college, with John Stuart Mill as the Law and the Gospel. It is what I have been reading for years in monthly bank letters. Always I am told that the one need is balanced production. Then each group of producers is able to buy its share of the output of all the other groups; then production itself automatically finances consumption; one man's demand is another man's supply; they must balance. Don't interfere with the law of supply and demand, and everything will work itself out as well as is humanly possible.

'Bunk!'

Again he spoke aloud, this time with even greater impatience, for his own experience in commerce and in finance had convinced him that there is no foundation, in the actual world of business, for the views with which the Lawyer and the Professor had discouraged the Little Gray Man.

Whereupon, by way of emphasis, the Business Man stood up and paced the floor.

'All that stuff,' he continued, 'is shown up every day by the ordinary course of business. It is nothing more than a left-over from the *laissez-faire* system of economics. There is no sense in saying that, because the old economists found no answer to the economic riddle, no answer can be found; no sense in saying that, because communism and all the other revolutionary programmes offer no solution, no solution can be found; no sense in saying that what always has happened, always must happen.'

Ever since the Business Man had left college, he had found his experience at variance with economic theories. The reason, he had become convinced, was because there was something wrong with the theories. It was not merely because business men thought of short-term movements, while professors thought of long-term movements. At the very core of the old economics, as he saw it, were assumptions which *made* men hopeless, but assumptions which, happily, were contrary to fact. So he had rejected the Economics of Despair — the dismal science, with its complacent attitude toward the snail-like progress of those who labor and are heavy laden.

'Anyway,' he assured himself, as he started to get ready for luncheon, 'I did well to keep out of that discussion. There is no use getting mixed up in a smoking-room argument.'

Still he could not help feeling sorry that the enthusiasm of the Little Gray Man had been chilled.

While these thoughts had been occupying the Business Man, as he sat alone in the smoking-room, the Professor, the Lawyer, and the Gray Man, who had left the train in search of fresh air, heard the very problems which they had just been discussing, expounded more vigorously and picturesquely, if not more intelligently.

No sooner had the three men left the car than they walked to the end of the platform, and there, in an open square, directly west of the railroad station, they saw a motley crowd. In its center, standing on the rear seat of a battered Ford car, was a scowling, gesticulating, red-haired orator. His audience appeared to be made up largely of men out of work, men from the idle mills which could be seen in the distance, stretched along the tracks, and workmen from other factories, looking for something to do in the lunch hour. On the fringe of the crowd were passengers from the west-bound express who, with the Professor, the Lawyer, and the Gray Man, were seeking diversion and fresh air.

'Why are you men unemployed?' The Red-Haired Orator fairly hurled rhetorical questions at the crowd.

'Because there is depression in textiles, they tell you. Don't be deceived. Millions of other would-be workers are unemployed all over the country. The employers say it is because of the World War. Haven't they heard that the War is over? Was the depression of 1907 also due to the War? And the "overproduction" panic of 1893? Don't be deceived. Men are always thrown out of work because of the System, and always will be until the System itself is thrown out of work!'

Cheers. Clapping of hands. Shouting.

'That's the stuff!'

'You said it!'

'Bravo!'

'Why should you be turned out?' continued the speaker. 'Why should millions of other men be unable to "get work" when their families are suffering for necessaries of life and the factories are closed in which these very things can be produced? Why can't everybody have a plenty? Why can't this army of the unemployed go into the idle mills, mines, and factories, and produce with their own labor the things they require?'

"'Cause they don't own 'em,' called a husky voice from the middle of the crowd.

'Yes, because they don't own the factories, and so have no right to work there — nor anywhere else. Why? Because the System requires a standing army of unemployed, in order that the Masters may have extra hands when needed. That is why thousands of men and women must wait outside the factory gates through long, weary weeks or months, until the gates are opened and they are allowed to work. And how long will they be allowed to work? Only as long as it is profitable for the employers, and no longer. The employers are not in business for their health. They are in business for PROFIT.'

More applause; more shouts; more pushing to get near the wobbly Ford.

'My friends, don't be deceived. The issue is the old one; the profiteers versus the producers; those who take, against those who make. So long as we permit a handful of men to own the railroads, the mines, the steel mills, the factories, the packing houses, in which we work and whose products we consume, so long will we be plundered and gouged. *We* must own these industries. *We* must operate them to serve ourselves at cost. That is the Road to Plenty!

'Take to the Road!' he exhorted, bending over and slapping his knee.

'Enlist as soldiers of the common good!' he cried, slapping his knee harder still. 'Become volunteers for humanity! Working, struggling, striving always to rescue your fellows from the misery, the degrading poverty, the appalling slaughter that capitalism in its ruthless greed has brought upon the world. And be not dismayed when the Money Power tries to crush you.

'CRUSH! CRUSH! CRUSH!' cried the Orator, energetically mopping his brow and brushing his long red hair aside with his coat-sleeve. 'That is all you hear from the Great Government that is supposed to protect you — CRUSH! CRUSH! CRUSH! Representatives of the Department of Justice are here this very minute to crush ——

'Crush what? The Associated Manufacturers who want to make slaves of us? Oh, no, not at all!

'Crush the prostituted capitalist press which poisons the brains of its readers with lies? God forbid! Nothing so terrible as that.

'All your Government aims to crush is your right to think! Your right to speak! Your right to live a decent life! Your right to educate your children! Your right to free yourself from industrial oppression! Oh, Hail to Justice!

'Read this morning's *Bulletin* — organ of the oppressors. Here it is; headline on the first page. "GREATEST ERA OF PROSPERITY. PRODUCTION OF WEALTH BREAKS ALL RECORDS." Who created all this wealth?'

'*We* did! WE DID!' Cries from the crowd.

'Well, then, who got it?'

'The bloodsuckers, they got it!'

'To whom should it belong, if not to you? Why suffer and starve in the midst of this sea of products created by your own toil? Throw away your slavish respect for the law; take everything you need! Feed the hungry! Destroy your dirty hovels! Move into the luxurious palaces of the idle rich! Whosoever shall hinder you, remove him from your path!

'Legislative reforms will accomplish nothing for you. Capitalists and their hired lawyers will give you a little charity and a lot of advice, nothing more. You yourselves must act. One mighty, irresistible, and fearful weapon remains in your hands — a general strike. How can you hold back? Look around and ask yourselves how much blood the bourgeoisie have drunk all over the world. Note these senseless sheddings of blood, committed under the protection of shameless law. What are we afraid of? For us there is the choice between eternal slavery and bloody struggle. Our choice is made. We call all workers to a merciless war upon Capital and Government. Destroy the bloodsuckers! That is the Road to Plenty.'

Cheers.

More harangue.

Cries of 'All aboard!'

SECTION IV

IN WHICH THE GRAY MAN FINDS A NEW HOPE

THE waiter stood by, expectant, but the unhappy Little Gray Man noticed nothing. He was suffering anew the disappointments of a lifetime. Torn open again were old wounds of the spirit: like vinegar had been the words he had heard that day.

Himself discouraged, he had to admit that his inspiriting good-byes to the discouraged mill hands were born of nothing but his own hope. As far as he could see, all that the young Burnses of this world had before them was to grow up — if, indeed, they could manage to grow up — and rear another generation of anxious, struggling families; and beyond that, still another generation, to be comforted with the thought that they were suffering 'only the usual volume of unemployment.' How many, many times he had heard men say, 'No use getting wrought up over the situation. Not much you can do about it!' Such smug complacency over other people's misfortune always came nearer than anything else to breaking down the universal tolerance of the Little Gray Man.

As far as he could see, none of the men in the smoking-room, neither the stupid nor the intelligent, had anything to offer that looked like a ray of hope for Joe Burns and thousands upon thousands in similar plight. Meantime, the Red-Haired Orator and his whole inflammatory tribe had a great deal to offer, and they were busy offering it, plausibly, persuasively. Yet, as the Gray Man was aware, what they offered would only make matters worse.

Still, it was something. And it was certainly far-reaching. Moreover, it did not dodge the main issue. It held as self-evident the truth that any economic system is intolerable which denies to millions of willing workers a chance to work.

'No more than the usual unemployment.' Small comfort that to Joe Burns! And no answer at all to the charges of the Red-Haired Orator. With firebrands like that around, how long could the complacent conservatives expect to keep the sparks out of the dry timber?

What was he, himself, to do? Go on the rest of his life, handing out what pitiful relief he could, and trying to convince the sufferers that there was hope, when there was no hope?

Absorbed in his thoughts and torn by his feelings, the Gray Man had not even noticed that some one had taken the seat across the table. When he looked up, he found himself face to face with the tall man who, during the discussion, had sat in the corner without speaking.

The Business Man nodded in friendly recognition. 'Quite a discussion this morning,' he said.

'Yes. I thought you looked interested.'

'I am always interested when men talk that way. For my part, I have never been able to understand how professors can speak with such finality about matters of business, or what lawyers have ever done to justify their scorn of mere business men.'

'And for my part, I hate to accept what such men say, but I can't see what is wrong with it.'

'I can.'

'What!' exclaimed the Gray Man. 'You don't agree with their hopeless views!'

'I certainly do not. They are not in accord with the experience of business men.'

At once the Gray Man was aroused. 'Do you mean to say,' he asked, 'that there is a practical way out, which those men have overlooked?'

'I certainly do.'

'Gr-e-a-t Jupiter! Let me hear it! I don't know when I have been so discouraged.'

Naturally buoyant in disposition, and now face to face with a man who inspired confidence, the Gray Man found his spirits rising. 'So you disagreed with those men, and yet kept still,' he said, incredulously. 'How could you do it? It goes all against my grain to accept their hopeless conclusions.'

'All against mine, too; but it is also against my grain to be dragged into smoking-car discussions. They seldom get anywhere.'

'That may be,' conceded the Gray Man. 'I suppose you are right. — Still — I wonder ——'

He stared, unseeing, at the flying telegraph poles. One question had all his attention: Can it be possible, after all my disappointments, that here is some one who really knows?

Then, turning to the Business Man, he asked, 'If, as you say, there is a way out, why has it never been tried?'

'For the very reason,' came the prompt answer, 'that

lawyers and professors hold the views you have just
heard. The facts which I have in mind, facts which these
men overlook, are the common knowledge of business
men, but business men say little and are prone to accept
the theories of lawyers and professors who, in turn, get
their main ideas, not enough from what is going on to-
day, but too largely from books — books which the professors write chiefly for each other. Nevertheless these
men, men of the type you heard this morning are influential. I fancy nothing of the sort I have in mind is likely to
be done until such men are convinced.'

Again the Gray Man stared at the flying telegraph
poles without seeing them. This time he was engrossed
with a new idea — a project which had just come to him.
Yes, he decided, it is worth trying.

'If that is the case,' he asked, 'why not try to convince
these two men? They are intelligent and serious-minded.
There they are now, so absorbed in some weighty argument that they are forgetting to eat their luncheon. I
feel sure that they would be glad to hear your ideas,
glad to tackle the whole subject, and stay with it all the
way to Chicago.'

'Possibly, but that looks like a highly speculative investment of time.'

'Still, the stakes are high,' urged the Gray Man.
'Fathers and mothers who struggle on the edge of poverty — millions who want work and cannot get it — aged
people in destitution. Can anything be better worth the
risk of a few hours' time?'

'But all that,' answered the Business Man, 'is part of a
complicated subject. No use discussing it casually. This

morning I felt sure that if I started to express my ideas, they would be brushed aside by some superficial remark. Then, again, I have little regard for reformers; I doubt if preaching ever does much good. Anyhow, I don't want to spend *my* life that way. I dislike talking about a serious matter unless there is a fair chance of getting somewhere.'

'Isn't it possible that this is just such a chance? Anyway, I hope you will show *me* a way out of the economic muddle.'

The Business Man said he had nothing in particular to do, his wife was taking a nap in the drawing-room, and he had no objection to going back to the smoking-room and continuing their talk. The truth was, he liked the Little Gray Man; admired his sincerity, his simplicity, his passion for helping the under-dog.

'What gets me,' said the Gray Man, earnestly, as soon as they were seated in the smoking-room, 'is the fact that with all our boasted prosperity, so many people still suffer from want and anxiety. As I was leaving the station this morning, Joe Burns exclaimed, "Give us back the good old war days, when everybody who wanted a job could get one!" And read this. I just tore it out of the *Times*.'

The Business Man read:

The Charity Organization Society has recently had such an unexpected increase of families coming to it asking for the bare necessities of life that this week an Emergency Relief Committee was appointed to consider ways and means of meeting this challenging situation.

'And that is in New York City,' commented the Gray Man.

'I know what it means,' said the Business Man. 'I happen to be a trustee of the Franklin Home for Aged Couples, and last month, when we had room for one new couple, it certainly was distressing to see all the pitiful grandfathers and grandmothers who came hobbling in to beg for that one place.'

'Then again,' the Gray Man added, 'with all our excess capacity for production, even those who *do* have jobs and are able to work — a majority of them, at least — cannot buy what millions of other people regard as common necessities.'

'Yes, I know.'

'But you can't possibly know, unless at some time you yourself have had no job, no money, no prospect of either, and at the same time somebody you love dependent on you. There is the case of Martin Barker, for example. In the depression of 1907 he was thrown out of work. His concern was overstocked from cellar to roof; had to shut down. So Martin was unemployed for six months. I give you my word, he was willing to do anything; there simply wasn't anything, except odd jobs now and then, that fell far short of feeding his family. So there he was — savings gone, rent months overdue, wife ill, children hungry, and no relief in sight. He had to see his children suffer, or else he had to beg or steal. He stole; and that is what I should have done in his place.'

After a pause, the Gray Man continued, 'It happens that Martin stole from the company that had discharged him — the Carlow Company. At a moment ——'

'What, the Carlow Company of Worcester?'

'Yes, Worcester. At a moment of desperation he found a way of supplying his immediate needs by theft. Never mind the details. Cases like that are common enough. Well, Martin went to jail. Anxious to desperation about his family before that, imagine his state of mind in jail. There he was a month later, when he heard of his wife's death.'

'But surely,' said the Business Man, plainly aroused, 'the President of the Carlow Company did not know those facts.'

'Oh, yes, he did; but he said he felt obliged to let the law take its course; said it would be a bad example to let a thief off too easily.'

'What a pity,' murmured the Business Man. 'I can't believe the President really understood the case.'

'Never mind the President. I don't blame him. No doubt the thief should have gone to jail. But what made that man a thief? An economic system which broke down and denied him a chance to work. That is the point. Do you blame him for crying out against such a system — a system which forces a man to commit crime or stand idly by and see his children suffer, for no fault of theirs and no fault of his? I say it is intolerable, if there is any possible remedy. And it seems to me there *must* be a remedy, because it is a fact that a case like Martin's could not have happened during the War, when there were jobs for everybody. Surely, there must be some way to prosper other than going to war.'

'It *is* intolerable,' agreed the Business Man.

'Well, then, why aren't you willing to tell us what can be done to develop a system which *is* tolerable?'

'I should have no objection to trying, if I thought that those men really wanted to discuss the matter seriously, and stay with it long enough to get down to brass tacks. Any other kind of a discussion would get nowhere.'

'Of course,' said the Gray Man, 'but you don't meet people on every train as thoughtful as the Professor and the Lawyer. And you say they are just the kind of men who must be reached before anything is likely to be done about it.'

The Business Man admitted that if it were possible to convince the Lawyer and the Professor that practical measures were readily at hand, such measures might be adopted; since those men appeared to be representative of large groups who are influential enough to bring about action or to prevent action.

'Here they are now,' exclaimed the Gray Man. Then, addressing them, he said, 'I was not at *all* reconciled to your conclusions before lunch; and the Red-Haired Orator made me feel worse. *He*, at least, had *some* kind of plan for discontented men to rally around.'

The Lawyer lighted a cigar and the Professor filled his brier pipe, while the Gray Man continued: 'I couldn't answer you myself, but here is a man who may be able to answer you out of his own experience. I know how successful he has been, and how widely acquainted at first hand with various industries, through his directorship in banks and corporations. Just as you came in, I was urging him to take up the discussion where we left off.'

'At least,' said the Business Man, 'you made me think, and that is hard work.'

'Hardest kind of work,' the Professor assented. 'When

I went to see Edison one day, I found a motto over his door: "There are no pains too great for mankind to take to avoid the trouble of thinking."'

'Well,' said the Business Man, 'I couldn't avoid that trouble, while hearing your talk.'

'Now it's your turn to make *us* think,' persisted the Gray Man.

'You can lead a man to college, but you cannot make him think,' observed the Professor. 'However, Pullman cars may not be hampered by traditions and alumni.'

'Not hampered by anything, according to our Little Gray Man, as I heard you call him. He seems to think that we have nothing better to do all the way to Chicago than wrestle with economic problems.'

'It's meat and drink to me,' the Professor remarked.

'No objection at all,' agreed the Lawyer.

'There you are,' cried the Gray Man. 'Now, go ahead and make us think, if you can; and make us think to some purpose. I have heard no end of discussions of the sort we had this morning; and always, like old Omar Khayyám, I come out by the same door wherein I went. Still, I think the whole situation doesn't make sense. There *must* be a way out.'

'There's always a way out: Lesson Number Seven in my correspondence course in Salesmanship.'

This remark was thrown in by the short, stout man in the checkered suit, who had entered the room while the Gray Man was speaking. Shaped like the earth, he was shining and flat at the north pole, and divided at the equator by a stout brown belt. No imaginary line, that!

He was not cast for vaudeville, as one might have supposed, but for the comedy of real life.

He was, in fact, as he informed the group without any urging, a past President of the Sure-Fire Sales Shooters of Chicago, and top-notch salesman for Sheer-Silk Hosiery, having won the March contest with a rank of ninety-three and a half per cent. That reminded him of the story about the procession of royalty of every rank, the rankest in front; and that reminded him of the story about the Scotchman's first ride in an aeroplane.

'And that reminds me,' he ran on, 'of the story about the blind beggar. Stop me if you've heard this one.'

And they did stop him, for at that moment the Kindly Lawyer, who had taken advantage of the interruption to go to the next car, now returned and introduced a friend from Kansas, an alert man with a smooth, round, rosy face, and a merry twinkle in his blue eyes. He was dressed in a coarse, brown tweed suit, which presumably once was new, but which certainly never did fit.

'I saw the Congressman at luncheon,' said the Lawyer. 'So, as soon as we decided to go on discussing business, I thought I ought to bring him in.'

'Nothing could be better,' the Business Man agreed, 'for the United States Government is the largest business in the world.'

'Well,' said the Gray Man, 'let's grapple with the problem, lock, stock, and barrel, and let's *stay* with it. Our Sure-Fire Shooter here, I am sure, will not mind postponing his target practice until after dinner.'

'I get you,' grinned the Sheer-Silk Salesman.

'For my own part,' continued the Gray Man, 'I am frankly bewildered, as I was saying in the dining-car. Nearly everybody wants more of the good things of life; I know thousands who are *suffering* for want of more, even in these prosperous times; and we were never so well equipped to produce more. Yet all along the road to-day we have seen closed factories; and right now millions of workers are without jobs, or on part time, because they have produced too much. It looks to me as though we all work hard to pile the shelves full of goods which we very much desire, and then have to stop working because we can't get rid of the goods. And whenever it is *especially* difficult to sell the goods, we make matters worse by reducing wages. We blame wage-earners for extravagant buying — the Bond Salesman's complaint is what you hear everywhere — and then we throw them out of work because enough goods have not been bought. Isn't that what we do, Professor?'

'No one can deny that it looks like that on the surface,' answered the Professor, with a smile.

'And no one can deny,' added the Congressman, 'that there is something puzzling about a world in which a bumper cotton crop is regarded as a national calamity. You can see how a big crop might worry the growers, but why does it have to throw the whole country into gloom? We work hard to produce abundantly, and when we succeed, we fall down on our knees and cry, "Lord, have mercy upon us and send us the boll-weevil, so we can prosper."'

'Another thing I never could understand,' said the Gray Man, 'is the foreign trade side of it. They tell me the *more* wealth we send abroad and the *less* we get in return, the more *favorable* is our balance of trade.'

In his earnestness, he was underscoring his chief words with even more than usual vigor. 'Here we are, *millions* of us,' he went on, 'eager for most of the things we send abroad; eager, also, for the things which the people abroad are eager to send *us;* yet we are always trying to force more goods on them, without taking payment in goods.'

'Haven't you heard,' asked the Congressman, with characteristic merriment in his eyes, 'that it is more blessed to give than to receive?'

'I have puzzled over all that,' said the Business Man, 'ever since I began to find out that actual business does not square with what I was taught in college. I am convinced now that traditional economic theory did not see the facts, partly because it was blinded by false assumptions. I have been getting more and more hopeful that all we need to do, in order to find a way out of the confusion, is to start with a few Plain Facts that everybody must accept, facts well known to business men.

'Now,' he added, 'shall I go on? Do you really want to run the risk of being bored?'

'I'm all for hunting the Plain Facts,' answered the Gray Man, 'if there really *are* any such animals in the economic wilderness.'

'Can't make 'em too plain to suit me,' nodded the Sheer-Silk Salesman. 'Tried to read a book on economics one time: all I got out of it was a headache. While you're at it, might tell me what to do with a guy who won't take a job when you hand him one. Sick of supportin' that

Socialist brother-in-law of mine; insists that the world owes him a livin'. Wish he wouldn't take *me* for the world, just 'cause I'm round. Plain Facts? As I says before, can't make 'em too plain for me.'

'The discussion will interest me,' said the Lawyer.

'Well, then,' the Congressman suggested, 'let's form a branch of the famous Skeptics' Society and proceed to investigate the question whether a Pullman-car conversation *has* to be as flat and barren as an Arizona desert.'

'Or as the *Congressional Record*,' added the Sheer-Silk Salesman.

SECTION V

'PERHAPS our discussion will be dull,' said the Business
Man, genially; 'but at least it won't be dull because we
agree on everything. To begin with, Professor, I believe
you said this morning that there is something in human
nature which makes extreme business depressions inevitable. I don't agree. You also said, I if remember correctly, that economic laws govern business cycles.'

'Virtually that.'

'Well, I don't believe that, either. To my mind, it is
mainly the decisions men make which determine the conditions under which economic laws operate; and those
decisions of men, rather than laws, determine whether
we have good times or bad times. But we can have good
times all the time if we make the right use of our savings.'

'Make the right use of our savings!' exclaimed the
Lawyer, with more scorn and astonishment than he often
allowed himself to show. 'I see nothing new in that idea.'

'Then our discussion may be dull, after all,' replied the
Business Man, with a quizzical smile, 'for that idea is the
heart of what I have to say.'

Not much in that, thought the Professor. What is the
use of trying to have a serious discussion with a man whose
main idea is the perfectly obvious fact that we have to
make use of our savings?

Then, turning to the Business Man, he said in his classroom tone of voice, 'If you mean that we can avoid business depressions merely by making the right use of our savings, I fear that you have not gone deeply enough into fundamental causes.'

'So here we are, with clash enough for a real fight!' exclaimed the Congressman, his face lighting up with mirth. 'Take my word, it makes me feel at home.'

'If it ain't a private fight, as the Irishman said, perhaps we can *all* have a good time.' The Sheer-Silk Salesman decided to postpone pinochle a little longer.

'And if your clash with the Professor is not enough, no doubt you will take issue with the Lawyer,' suggested the Gray Man.

'Especially,' answered the Business Man, turning to the Lawyer, 'I take issue with the view I understood you to express this morning, that about all we need to keep us prosperous is balanced production. By balanced production I suppose you mean the right volume of plate glass, tires, and automobiles, in relation to each other, and to other products — sheer-silk hosiery and all the rest; not too much of any one thing, compared with the output of other things. Such a balanced condition, I grant you, is much to be desired; but it is far from enough. The people of China could have balanced production and die of poverty. Even if it were possible in this country — as it is not — to attain perfectly balanced production, the problem would still be unsolved. But we *can* solve it by making the right use of our savings. Let me ——'

'Merely repeating that remark does not invest it with meaning for me,' interrupted the Lawyer.

'What I mean is *saving for use, and not for waste.* If you will bear that in mind, and be patient, I will develop the idea.'

'We can be patient more easily,' suggested the Professor, 'if you will state the essentials of your solution at the outset. That will make it easier to follow your argument.' The Professor refrained from adding, 'if you really have an argument.'

'Yes,' agreed the Gray Man, although he did not share the academic scorn, 'I can hardly wait to find out what you propose to do about it.'

The Business Man knew that the best statement he could make, under the circumstances, would not be clear to any one. He would have to be brief, that was certain; and a brief explanation would necessarily fail to answer many pertinent questions. So he decided not to disclose his position until he had prepared the way by reminding his hearers of certain facts, well-known to them, which they would have to take into account in order to understand his plan.

'First let me remind you,' he said, 'that business goes up and then goes down. When it goes up, as you all know, demand grows faster than supply, and prices rise. People rush into the markets and try to buy more goods than the markets afford. Business booms. So manufacturers pay more wages, make more goods, build more equipment, place orders further ahead, and speculate in commodities, all of which causes a further rise in prices, a further expansion of industry, and so on.'

'That is what we call a vicious spiral of inflation,' commented the Professor.

'Say,' interrupted the Sheer-Silk Salesman, 'if that's what you call economics, I oughter be a professor. My father learned me all that in his store on Hanover Street, before I was big enough to tell a real fire from an insurance fire.'

'Did he also learn you, old Semi-Silk Salesman,' asked the Congressman, with the lustrous look in his eyes, 'that there are other times when goods flow to market faster than money?'

'Didn't have to learn me that, old Semi-Sane Solon. Saw it myself.'

'Then you saw goods pile up on the shelves and prices fall,' resumed the Business Man. 'Things went from bad to worse. The movement did not correct itself, because falling prices usually are so discouraging that business men discharge workers, reduce wages, curtail output, postpone additions to plant, buy only from hand to mouth, and keep down their inventories, all of which causes a further fall in consumer income and a further fall in prices. That leads, naturally, to a further retrenchment of business, a further fall in wages and dividends, a further fall in prices, and so on.'

'And that is what we call a vicious spiral of *deflation*,' said the Professor. 'All well-known to economists.'

'From all of which comes my main conclusion.'

'Which is?'

'That under present conditions, business is certain to get well started either up or down, and either way the end is hard times. Corrective influences do not automatically restore the equilibrium, except far too slowly and at the tragic cost of human suffering. No matter which way business is headed, all forces combine to accelerate the movement. There is not an even chance that either inflation or deflation, once well under way, will be stopped in time, without more effective efforts to stop it than we have ever made in the past. Isn't that the case, Professor?'

'Yes, I suppose I must agree with you on that point.'

'At least,' said the Lawyer, 'we must all agree that each individual is prompted in his own interests to do precisely what makes matters worse. If inflation is under way, he expects further inflation. So he orders more goods, enlarges production, expands facilities; in short, helps along the upward movement. If deflation is under way, he expects further deflation. So he reduces production, postpones buying, lays off workers, pays off bank loans; in short, does precisely what will help along the downward movement.'

'Just what some of the largest railroads did last summer,' commented the Congressman. 'As soon as they found that business was falling off, they curtailed their own development programmes, thus making business worse still.'

'Exactly,' the Business Man agreed. 'But why? If we miss the reason why men act in that way, we miss the key to the problem. Each man acts as he does because he feels pretty sure that there will be no effective effort to stop the movement. And note that, as long as nothing is done to stop it, each man really does pursue his own interests by following policies which ultimately prove contrary to the interests of all.'

'I am not sure that I get your full meaning,' said the

Professor, doubtfully. 'Do you contend that as long as we rely on individual initiative, there is little chance of making steady progress?'

'Little chance? Say, rather, no chance at all. Consider these facts: At present, no individual has any responsibility for the general situation; nor has he, as a rule, any means of knowing what the general situation calls for. It is not to be expected that the independent acts of hundreds of thousands of such men, each following what seems to him to be his own interests, will together make the right use of our savings to promote the common good.'

'Which last remark,' commented the Professor, 'is contrary to classical economics.'

'Because, as I may possibly convince you, classical economics is wrong.'

'So you think that the "Beneficent Hand" itself needs guidance?'

'I certainly do. I feel sure that I can propose measures which will enable us to deal with the situation. Individual initiative must, of course, be preserved; nothing whatever should be done to interfere with that. Now, however, it is actually for the interests of individuals to do what, resulting in depression, turns out to be contrary to the interests of business as a whole. But we can establish conditions under which each individual can best pursue his own interests by doing what is for the interests of all.'

'The trouble is,' said the Congressman, 'that we never know what is going on until it is too late to take the necessary remedial measures, even if we knew what measures to take. A business depression gets well under way before there are any concerted efforts, public or private, to check the movement.'

'And yet,' the Business Man declared emphatically, 'the whole situation is very largely subject to our control.'

'Go to it!' applauded the Gray Man. 'That is what I have been wanting to hear.'

'Too simple an explanation, I fear,' said the Lawyer.

'Too simple so far,' echoed the Professor scornfully, turning up his nose with a rabbit-like sniff. ' But as you proceed, I suppose you will take more account of established economic doctrines. I admit that most professors are too much out of touch with actual business; and you will admit, no doubt, that business men, as a rule, are not well versed in economic theory. They are inclined to draw sweeping conclusions from their own experiences — rule of thumb procedure, necessarily rather narrow — and their views are consequently rather superficial.'

'Entirely natural for you to take such a position,' smiled the Business Man, unoffended. 'I did not expect you to accept my unsupported statement. I have thrown it out in bald form because you said you wanted to see, at the outset, where I was headed.'

'Now,' said the Professor, 'I for one shall be glad to have you develop your plan — the Business Man's Theory of Progress, I suppose we should call it.'

'Very well, if you like, we can now consider the Plain Facts on which you will find that the theory is based.'

SECTION VI

IN WHICH A FEW PLAIN FACTS ARE USED AS MILESTONES

'AT least, you will agree to one thing,' said the Business Man, good-naturedly, already half-prepared to thank the Little Gray Man for getting him into this discussion. 'At least you will agree that we have abundant production facilities; there is no lack of savings. That, perhaps, is as good a Plain Fact as any to start with.'

'Even Joe Burns knows that,' commented the Gray Man. 'Even the Red-Haired Orator mentioned it.'

'And every industry with which any one of you is acquainted goes to prove it,' continued the Business Man. 'Nevertheless, everybody keeps on preaching thrift. How to increase our savings is even said to be the country's chief economic problem. As a matter of fact, from the national standpoint, that is no problem at all. Already we have saved far more than we use. How to make use of our savings is the real problem.'

'It is a fact,' conceded the Lawyer, 'that nearly every industry is oversupplied with savings. In some cases the excess capacity is notorious — textiles, coal, tires, iron, steel, shoes ——'

'Cotton, corn, wheat, fruit,' the Congressman added. 'Don't leave out the farmers.'

'And the knitting industries. Don't forget us,' said the Semi-Silk Salesman.

'Yes,' continued the Business Man, 'the list covers the whole range of industrial life, the world over.

But the Professor could not let such vague statements go unchallenged. 'Some of these wastes of capital,' he observed, 'cannot be prevented. Some of our unused savings are in the form of obsolete machinery, too costly to use, anyway. Other capital savings are unused at times because they are needed only to carry peak loads, or are designed to take care of growth. Still other capital is idle because fashions change; or because somebody has set up machinery for producing what nobody will buy at profit-yielding prices; or because some industry — like the textile industry to-day — is relatively over-equipped. In such cases there is not too much capital savings, but the wrong kinds.'

'Of course there always must be such cases in every progressive society,' the Business Man replied. 'But I am not talking about such cases. That is not what I mean by wasted savings. What I mean is the well-known fact that nearly all industries — not exceptional ones, but nearly all — are now equipped to increase the output of the very goods which the people want. That is a far different thing from relative over-equipment. All industries cannot be relatively over-equipped at the same time.'

'No need of arguing that point,' the Congressman insisted. 'Everybody knows that most of our industries could increase their output twenty per cent, thirty per cent, in some cases fifty per cent or more, with their present labor force working full time, if — this is the big IF — IF both the employers and the employed could do their best and keep on doing it.'

'The War taught us that,' added the Lawyer. 'After it had thrown industry into confusion and taken four million workers away from their jobs, the workers who were left produced enough to supply all the wealth which was sunk at sea and blown up in battle, enough to supply our own Army and Navy and millions of people abroad, and enough more to enable the people at home to enjoy at least as high a standard of living as before the War.'

The Business Man urged the Professor to bear in mind that whenever he spoke of unused capacity, he was not referring to facilities that were out of use for any of the reasons which had just been mentioned, nor to that part of our total facilities which would have to remain unused, in any event, because of a limited supply of labor. The Professor, on his part, admitted that after leaving out of account all such cases of idle capital, there remains a great wealth of capital which is not used at any approach to capacity even by our most successful companies. He cited General Motors as an example. 'An astounding instance of increased productivity,' he remarked, 'yet it does not count on using, normally, more than seventy per cent of its facilities. The country as a whole does not do as well as that, even in its best years.'

'How much greater is the waste, then, in our worst years!' the Gray Man exclaimed. 'Think of 1921, when our warehouses were bulging with leather, wool, cotton, lumber, copper, chemicals. Think of the four million idle workers who were eager to go to work. I ought to know how *they* felt. And think of the millions of people who were eager for the things which these idle workers, by the use of these idle machines, could readily make out of these surplus materials.'

'That sums up the situation,' said the Business Man.

'Machines, materials, men, and money in superabundance; hungry mouths to feed and every means of feeding them; willing hands to work and plenty to work with. Now, the question is, why could no immediate means be found of letting this stupendous wealth of machines, materials, men, and money go on with the world's work? If the means could be found, year in and year out, the output of industry could be doubled. Isn't that so, Professor?'

'Some people would say,' answered the Professor, 'that we need, not more goods, but a better quality of goods. However, we are perfectly able to produce both better goods and more of them. That is evident from the great advances we have made in the arts.'

'Also in power development,' added the Congressman, 'as well as in scientific management, reduction of wastes, and public health. The advance of knowledge alone ought to give us more goods and better goods, and consequently far higher standards of living.'

'That being the case,' said the Business Man, 'do you not begin to see some sense in my first remarks about thrift? Saving is, of course, a worthy habit, an ancient virtue. Individuals must save, or go to the Poor House; corporations must save, or go bankrupt. And evidently we have saved — saved with prodigality, if I may use a word heretofore applied only to spending. That is to say, we have saved far more in productive facilities than we have yet found out how to use. We are *wasting* our savings, whereas it is only in so far as we *use* our savings that we make progress. People are constantly saving and investing, only to find that their savings are lost because they are turned into capital which cannot be used.'

'That's me,' the Semi-Silk Salesman cried, with feeling. 'Socialist brother-in-law says, better give him my money. No use investing it. Generally turns out he's right.'

'It is the problem of society,' continued the Business Man, 'to make effective use of the people's savings. Wasting them destroys incentives to save; for who feels like saving more, when he has lost his past savings by investing them in capital which cannot be used?'

'Nobody,' declared the Gray Man. 'I can tell you out of abundant experience that nothing would do more to encourage thrift than to make effective use of savings, once they are made ——'

'Do you fancy,' the Professor asked, with his rabbit-like sniff, 'that you can prevent every fool from investing his savings in Florida lots at a dollar a gallon?'

'Did you never lose any of your own invested savings?' replied the Business Man. 'Yet you are nobody's fool. As things go now, some large losses *must* come about, not through the folly of individual investors, but largely, as I hope to convince you, because at present there is no way of fully using and steadily using even such of our capital savings as are well conceived and well distributed. And much of the losses which are due to that cause *can* be prevented.'

'Isn't that a challenge!' exclaimed the Gray Man. 'With all our unused facilities for producing wealth, doesn't it seem stupid to sit by, content with a progress which is forever shadowed by poverty! Is it right for those who have powers of leadership to duck all responsibility by saying that there is not much of anything we can do about it?'

'All we need to do, apparently,' said the Business Man, 'is to supply whatever is now lacking to enable us to use our savings.'

'Well,' asked the Gray Man, 'what is it that is now lacking? With all these unused facilities at our command, why don't we produce a plenty? One thing I know; there is no lack of desire. Can't we put that down as a Second Plain Fact? The people eagerly want more of the good things of life, and there are not enough to go around.'

'That is a fundamental fact,' the Professor agreed.

'Equally plain,' continued the Gray Man, 'is a Third Fact: the fact that even in our prosperous country, most of the people would be much better off if they had more wealth; not merely better off in bodily comfort — though Heaven knows that is needed badly enough — but better off, as well, in all else that makes life worth living.'

'No one can question that fact,' declared the Congressman, 'when ten million families are suffering for lack of necessities, or struggling anxiously on the edge of want.'

'And ten million other families,' the Gray Man added, 'though not in such dire need, are nevertheless forced to get along without half enough income to maintain the standard of living which you men regard, for your families, as the barest requirement for health and decency, to say nothing of comfort and security.'

'And how much worse off the people are in nearly every other country on earth!' said the Lawyer.

'You don't need to convince me,' declared the Congressman. 'It is the well-to-do who need convincing. For them the tragedy of the poor is a closed book. To them this world seems a pretty good place to live in, just about as it is; they see no reason for stirring up people to change it. Too bad they can't have a Little Gray Man to open their eyes. Then they might find statistics quickened into life. They might realize that most human beings are very much like themselves, and so must have more of the things that money will buy, before they can make gains in the refined pleasures of life.'

'No doubt,' said the Gray Man, 'the voluntary *over*-consumption of the rich and foolish is not conducive to the higher life. If the Bishop had confined his sermon to them, I could have agreed with him. But neither is there anything spiritually uplifting in the *under*consumption of the millions who have no choice. Malnutrition, child labor, crowded tenements, disease, ignorance, fear of destitution — all the evils that go with poverty; ye gods, how they haunt me, night and day!'

'Of course, you are right.' The Congressman spoke with warmth and vigor. It was clear that he fully shared the Gray Man's urge to action. 'Nearly everybody needs more of the things that money will buy. The question is, why must we struggle along so slowly? Why must we wait another hundred years before we find the Road to Plenty?'

'That question,' said the Business Man, 'brings us to another Plain Fact. This must be the Fourth one in our list. Nobody can enjoy oranges which are not grown, or dresses which are not made. We cannot have a plenty unless we create a plenty.'

'But we could make the wage-earners a lot better off,'

the Gray Man observed, 'if we gave them larger shares of what we *do* produce.'

'Still,' objected the Lawyer, 'the gain would be slight. Even if all the wealth that is annually consumed in this country were divided equally, and even if we still had enough savings in new capital, wage-earners as a whole would be little better off. I agree that a reduction of the glaring inequalities of income would be good for everybody, the rich included, especially their children; but that is not enough. The only way to give the people much more of the good things of life is to produce much more.'

The Little Gray Man refrained from suggesting that the Lawyer, if he were in the plight of Joe Burns, might not be so complacent about the uneven distribution of wealth. Instead, he asked, 'What if we did produce more? Most of it would not go to the people who need it most.'

'That raises another problem,' the Business Man replied. 'A very important one, not to be solved by leaving it alone; but to discuss it now, would take us too far afield. For our present purposes it is enough to note the fact that those who are in greatest need certainly would gain largely if there were large gains in the total per capita output. That is what always happens. Whether they would enjoy as large a proportion of the increase as we should like to have them enjoy is another question.'

'Well, then,' the Gray Man asked, 'why *don't* we produce more? We have all agreed that there are plenty of facilities. Why don't we use them?'

'Right here,' answered the Business Man, 'our Sure-Fire Salesman is going to hit the bull's eye.'

Then, turning to the Salesman in the corner, the Business Man asked, 'Why doesn't your company produce more stockings?'

'That's an easy one. Because we can't sell more.'

'And why don't your competitors make more stockings?'

'Because *they* can't sell more, of course.'

'Are you sure that is the only reason?'

'Am I sure of that? Say, I wish I had as many dollars as I'm sure of that.'

'Of course you are right,' assented the Business Man. 'And all the other Sure-Fire Sales Shooters would tell the same story. This, then, is a Fifth Plain Fact: The only reason the business world does not produce more is because it cannot sell more. Lack of markets is the trouble. We never produce a plenty for fear of producing too much.'

'Say,' exclaimed the Semi-Disgusted Salesman, 'everybody knows that. Thought you said you were goin' to talk economics; haven't said a thing yet to give a feller a headache. Even that fool salesman for cough drops could follow you — Jake — er — what's his name? Funny I can't remember it. Tryin' all mornin' get me to play pinochle, car ahead. Jake — er — er —— Anyway, he says, "Sam, if only my customers was all giraffes." And I says ——'

'Yes,' interrupted the Congressman, 'and you says, " If only my customers was all centipedes!" But let's go on with the discussion. We were just remarking that business never produces a plenty for fear of producing too much.'

'But why?' the Gray Man asked, still pursuing the basic trouble, while the Salesman in the corner was mumbling through the alphabet in pursuit of Jake's last name. 'Why must the whole world fear *over*production, when millions are suffering from *under*consumption?'

'It does seem incomprehensible, on first thought,' commented the Business Man. 'Yet on second thought it seems plain enough. "Overproduction," "underconsumption," "lack of markets" — those are only different names for the same condition — the plight of business without a buyer.'

'You mean,' said the Congressman, 'that there is no sense in raising more hogs, when we can't make any money on the hogs we have already raised; no use putting more furnaces into blast, when stocks of pig-iron are piling up.'

'And Joe Burns knows to his sorrow,' added the Gray Man, 'that the mills will not spin more cloth when there are no buyers for the cloth already spun.'

'In short,' the Business Man concluded, 'industry cannot go ahead turning out more goods until it can get rid of the goods which it has already turned out. We have previously agreed that the country is fully equipped to produce more goods; that the people want more, and ought to have more; and that they cannot have more unless they produce more. Now we have agreed to this Fifth Plain Fact: They cannot produce more unless they can sell more. That is the same as saying that in this money-and-profit world in which we have to do business — the only one, by the way, which has ever proved workable on a large scale — sales regulate consumption, and consumption regulates production.'

'But the slogan of the banks is, "Save more in order to have more,"' said the Congressman.

'Like most maxims,' answered the Business Man, 'that is only a half truth. The other half is that a community has to *consume* more in order to have more. So — note carefully — sales determine to what extent we can make use of our savings.'

'That is true, at any rate,' confirmed the Lawyer, 'of all the companies with which I am familiar. Lack of markets is the only reason why the General Electric Company does not turn out more lamps; the only reason why the International Harvester Company does not make more tractors. Nothing else restrains the Thor Company from making more washing machines, the Standard Sanitary Company from making more bathtubs, or the Sherwin-Williams Company from making more paint.'

The Professor, still trying to waterproof every statement, mentioned cases in which the limiting factor in supply is the number of competent workmen or the quantity of available materials. 'But such cases,' he added, 'are usually temporary; and always they are exceptional. Their influence on the gross volume of production is negligible. Without admitting that this helps your case at all, I do admit that, for the industrial world as a whole, except in periods of inflation, the limiting factor is the market.'

'We seem to agree, then,' said the Business Man, 'on a Fifth Plain Fact, to which all our other Plain Facts have led us: Ordinarily, the only reason why we do not, as producers, provide ourselves with more of what we want is because, as distributors, we cannot sell more. Let ——'

'In short,' commented the Lawyer, 'the one need of business is a buyer.'

'The papers always make a noise when buyers come to town; never show any interest in us,' remarked the Salesman.

'A significant fact,' the Business Man declared. 'Let it be known that there is a buyer at hand for any producible goods and the goods will be produced. That, and only in a minor degree patriotism, is the reason why we increased our output so greatly during the War. The fact is, the largest increase came at the demand of foreign buyers, before we entered the War.'

'Look out the window,' suggested the Congressman, 'and tell me what that handsome man with the cigarette is doing out there on the billboard. What are all the lovely women doing on all the other billboards? Begging us to buy the stuff which producers are ready and eager to supply.'

'That's it. The whole financial and industrial world is set up for the very purpose of doing whatever buyers direct it to do.'

'A willing buyer,' added the Congressman, 'never has to wait long, but a willing seller may have to wait forever.'

'Exactly,' said the Business Man. 'If any one of you should appear in Chicago to-morrow morning with plenty of money and an order for a thousand pairs of silk knee breeches with diamond buckles, the order would be filled promptly. It would be just as easy for you to have a hundred whaling vessels launched on Lake Michigan. If you wanted something which required new capital facilities, those facilities would be created. The investment world is always ready to provide money to be used in producing anything for which there is a manifest money demand.'

Just then a freight train roared by on the next track. The talking ceased, but the thinking went on. Thought the Salesman, this may point the way to something that will help the hosiery business. Thought the Congressman, can't yet see just where the Government comes in. Thought the Lawyer, there is much sense in all this, I must admit. Thought the Professor, here is another man who expects to cure all our ills by giving the people more money. How these wild men do bob up, year after year! This one will soon get beyond his depth.

But the Little Gray Man, keener than ever for stalking the Plain Facts, waited only for the last freight car to rumble by, when he cried, 'Sound the horns, and let the hunt go on.'

'The Plain Fact which we were discussing,' continued the Business Man, 'is that it is not poverty of productive power that restrains us from making greater gains in standards of living, but periodic lack of buyers. The next question is: Why this lack of buyers?'

'I think I can cover that point,' said the Gray Man. Then to the Porter who was shambling out of the room in an old pair of shoes, the Gray Man called: 'Why haven't you got a new pair of shoes this spring, George?'

'Nobody ain't left none on my car lately, suh.'

'Then why don't you *buy* a new pair?'

'Ain't got enough money, suh. That all's the reason.'

'Don't your tips average high enough?'

'Average is pow'rful good, suh. Mah average tip's a dollar; but, Lordy, ain't got as much as that but once all winter.'

'There you are,' chuckled the Congressman. 'The Porter doesn't have to take a course in economics to answer the question.'

'Neither do I,' said the Gray Man, ruefully. 'I know why *I* haven't stimulated producers to make more goods; solely because my income has not allowed me that pleasure. But I suppose, Professor, my answer is too simple to satisfy an economist.'

'Not at all,' responded the Professor, loyal to the truth, even at the cost of aiding the Business Man's case. 'Your answer is in accord both with common sense and common experience. It certainly squares with the experience of college professors.'

'As a matter of fact,' said the Business Man, 'the records show that fluctuations in the dollar volume of retail sales are almost identical with fluctuations in the dollar volume of wages. But nobody needs statistics to convince him that the buying of wage-earners increases about as rapidly as their incomes. Statistics merely confirm what everybody knows.'

'Still,' objected the Lawyer, trying to light a cigar from a patent device which he had taken from his waistcoat pocket, 'still, all the business and financial papers said the depression of 1920 began with a consumers' strike.'

'There never is any such thing as a consumers' strike,' the Gray Man asserted emphatically. 'When the people as a whole fail to buy, it is because they have no money.'

'Then they are not strikers,' said the Congressman; 'they should be classed with the unemployed.'

'Take the growth of installment selling,' added the Business Man. 'Doesn't that show that the country can produce more goods than people are able to buy and pay for? Houses, automobiles, books, pianos, washing machines, radios, oil heaters, all offered on easy terms.'

'Too easy, much too easy,' blustered the Semi-Silk Salesman. 'Bad for business. All these boobs payin' installments on tin lizzies and foldin' beds and false teeth, when they oughter be buyin' more silk stockin's.'

'You didn't buy a car on installments yourself, by any chance, did you?' asked the Congressman.

'Me!' the Semi-Silk Salesman exclaimed scornfully. 'Me pay nine per cent interest on deferred payments! Say, do you think I need a guardian?'

'No, a Maxim Silencer,' answered the Congressman. 'Let's get back to the point.'

'The point is,' continued the Business Man, 'that we have the ability, as producers, to create all this wealth. There it is before our eyes, already created. We have produced and turned over to consumers on installment sales at least three billion dollars' worth, in excess of what they have paid for. The very fact that we cannot get rid of what we make, even in these prosperous years, without persuading the people to mortgage their incomes further and further into the future, seems to show that the flow of money to people who want to buy goods does not keep pace with the flow of the goods.'

'And we must not forget,' added the Gray Man, 'that

everybody says a business depression is sure to come sooner or later. If would-be consumers can't buy the output even in these times, how much less can they buy, with two or three billions of installments still due, when another depression reduces their wages by seven billion dollars, and their income from other sources by many billion more.'

'You conclude, then,' summed up the Professor, 'that we cannot hope to use our capital savings or our labor continuously at any approach to capacity, unless individual incomes, week in and week out, are such that the people buy all the finished products of home industry, or the equivalent in imports, about as rapidly as they are ready for sale.'

'That's it, in a nutshell.'

'And with that much,' said the Professor, 'I largely agree. So far you are in accord with economists.'

'But in my next step, I am not. I conclude from these very facts that we must provide as effectively for financing consumption in the future, as in the past we have provided for financing production. As a rule, underconsumption is the chief trouble; therefore the right flow of money to consumers is the chief need. The question is, How can we get the right flow?'

'I must say,' declared the Congressman, 'you are talking a language I can understand.'

'Right you are, old Solon,' agreed the Semi-Silk Salesman. 'May be too simple for the Professor; gets me where I live.'

'So far,' the Lawyer assented, 'I, too, have had to accept your Plain Facts, one after another. Before I accept any more, I should like to know where they are leading me.'

'Naturally,' chuckled the Congressman. 'You don't want to be a turkey, eating a trail of corn with your head down, and at the end of the trail suddenly look up and find yourself caught in a coop. Nice place, that, for a lawyer.'

'So far,' the Business Man assured the Lawyer, 'you have been safe enough, picking up one kernel at a time. Now, let's see where we are. We have agreed that this country is fully equipped to increase the output of goods; that the country is, in fact, wasting much of its savings by investing them in productive facilities which cannot be used. Moreover, the people want and ought to have a plenty. They do not have a plenty because they do not create a plenty. They do not create it because it can't be sold. It can't be sold because consumers never long obtain the right amount of money for the purpose.'

'Why not?' asked the Lawyer. 'What prevents consumers from getting the needed money? That, I take it, is logically the next question. I have always supposed that in the long run the process of making goods automatically provided people with the right amount of money to buy the goods. At least ——'

'Works about as well as that automatic cigar-lighter you've been coaxin' for the last five minutes,' interrupted the Salesman. 'Here, before you go on, try a Sure-Fire match.'

SECTION VII

IN WHICH IT APPEARS THAT THE RIGHT USE OF OUR SAVINGS DEPENDS ON THE RIGHT FLOW OF MONEY TO CONSUMERS

'BEFORE we go on,' said the Business Man, turning to the Lawyer, 'I might tell you what you are thinking about.'

The Lawyer looked expectant.

'You are already thinking that it would be a mistake to try experiments at a time when the United States is more prosperous than ever before; in fact, the most prosperous country in the world. Let well enough alone. Don't run the risk of upsetting the whole apple cart, when it is heaped with fine, rosy apples. Am I right?'

'Right.'

'Furthermore, you are convinced that the established economic system works as well as could be expected. In the main, the right adjustment of supply and demand seems to come about automatically, as is shown by record-breaking production, real wages, savings, and so on.'

'Still right.'

'Under such circumstances, you hold that the safe course is to leave economic laws alone in the future, as in the past, to work things out for the common good. Anyway, the burden of proof is on those who advocate a change, not only because it is a change, but because the established system is delivering the goods.'

'I must say,' admitted the Lawyer, 'that you have well expressed my ideas.'

'That's nothin'!' exclaimed the Semi-Silk Salesman.
'I'm a mind-reader, too. Tell you what's on the Little
Gray Man's mind. Those ideas are bunk! That's what
he's thinkin'.'

'I assure you,' the Business Man continued, 'that I
shall take all those ideas into account, in due course.
But first let me try to answer your question: How does it
happen that consumers never long obtain the right
amount of money to buy the products of industry? Well,
where do consumers get their money anyway?'

'In the little pay envelope,' answered the Salesman.

'And as interest, dividends, and rent,' added the Lawyer.

'Yes,' said the Business Man, 'and that all comes
from industry — industry in its broadest sense, including
farming, banking, insurance, and transportation; industry
in the process of producing and distributing goods, and
industry in the process of creating facilities for producing
more goods. Consumers have no source of money other
than industry.'

'And the Government.' The Congressman talked as he
ran back and forth over the motley collection of papers
which he had taken from his stuffed pocket. 'Last year
the Federal Government spent about — yes, here are
the figures — in fact, spent over three billion dollars,
and state and local governments spent over seven billion
more. Nearly all that money went to consumers, didn't
it?'

'Let us not forget that for a moment,' urged the Business Man. 'We must also remember that industry, on
the other hand, has no source of income except consumers

— including the largest consumers of all, the federal, state, and local governments. Thus there is a constant flow of money from industry to consumers, and from consumers back to industry; and this stream is not fed by providential cloudbursts.'

'Not in Kansas, at any rate, and we are authorities on cloudbursts,' said the Congressman, decidedly. 'Take my word, they never bring down money.'

'Then,' the Business Man concluded, 'either industry gets enough money from consumers to keep prosperous, or industry does not get the money at all. On the other hand, either consumers get enough money from industry and from governments, to buy all the goods that industry puts upon the markets, or else consumers do not get the money at all.

'Now I'm lost again,' moaned the Semi-Silk Salesman, holding his head in both hands. 'Makes me dizzy to see so much money goin' round and round, and not be able to lay hands on it.'

'Anyway,' said the Business Man, 'you have the right idea. Money does go around in circles constantly. So, if business paid back to consumers all the money it received from consumers, and consumers spent all the money — that is to say, if there were no savings — there would be a steady circuit flow, and no trouble at all about selling a *given* volume of goods at a given level of prices.'

'You mean that two is equal to two, and always will be,' said the Congressman. 'I agree. Even the Professor might be willing to commit himself on that point.'

'But,' objected the Salesman, 'business *doesn't* pay out all the money it takes in; and people *don't* spend all they get — except such cheerful idiots as that brother-in-law of mine.'

'It is true,' the Business Man replied, 'that both corporations and individuals must save; yet if they do save, they cause a shortage of consumer buying, which has to be made up in some way, or business depression results. That is certainly a dilemma — the Dilemma of Thrift, we might call it.'

'And if business is to sell a constantly *increasing* output,' added the Congressman, 'the shortage due to savings must be *more* than made up. In other words, consumers must get back all the money they spend in any given period and more, too.'

'And so,' concluded the Professor, 'there is no possibility of raising the standard of living, while maintaining a stable price-level, without increasing the volume of money. I commit myself on that point, too.'

'That's plain English, anyway,' said the Congressman. 'But usually I can't understand professors. I've a hunch it's because they don't exactly understand themselves. Would you believe even a professor could go as far as this?' Again the Congressman fumbled through the papers which he must have been collecting, in his inside pocket, for at least two sessions of Congress. 'Here it is, a quotation from one of your highly regarded professors of economics: "If we are getting restless under the taxonomy of a monocotyledonous wage doctrine and a cryptogamic theory of interest, with involute, loculicidal, tomentous, and moniliform variants, what is the cyptoplasm, centrosome, or karyokinetic process to which we may turn, and in which we may find surcease from

the metaphysics of normality and controlling principles?"'

'That's a pippin!' exclaimed the Semi-Silk Salesman.
'Monocotygamic Theory of Karyo-ki-ki-kitchenettes.
Must remember that. Boss thinks only thing I know is
hosiery. I'll show him.'

'Meantime, returning to the subject ——' suggested
the Gray Man.

'The point is,' said the Business Man, 'that we cannot increase the standard of living, without increasing
the volume of money at the right rate. A very Plain
Fact it is, so plain that it has met the fate of the wall-
flower, while its fascinating and far from plain sister,
Marginal Utility, has been whirled around until many
men besides the Salesman have become dizzy.'

'Marginal Utility. Another pippin!' exclaimed the
Salesman. 'Must remember that, too. Not so good,
though, as Monocryptomentous Theory of Kitchenettes.'

The Professor, now at a loss to know which of his fellow
travelers was most in need of pity, wrinkled his forehead,
looked over his glasses at the Business Man, and said,
'There is nothing new in what you say about the need of
more money. Economists long ago laid down the maxim
that with a given volume of money in circulation, other
factors remaining the same, it is impossible for industry
to sell an increased volume of goods.'

'Without more money, then,' continued the Business
Man, 'those billboards out there, no matter how successful they may be in getting people to buy one thing
rather than another, cannot increase the total sales of
the country; nor can high-pressure salesmen, or opti-

mism, or balanced production, or improved labor relations, or any other factor. The question is not whether
a rising standard of living requires a growing volume of
money, but how the growth is to be brought about at
the right rate.'

'It is, of course, true,' said the Professor, still insisting
on qualifications, 'that even with a fixed volume of
money, larger sales could be made to consumers by means
of a fall in the price-level, or a faster circuit velocity of
money, or a piling-up of consumer debts. But otherwise,
with a given volume of money, it is possible to sell only
a given volume of goods, and no more.'

'Help! Help! I'm drownin'!' The Semi-Silk Salesman threw up his hands. 'That's worse than Marjorie's
Kitchenette.'

'Sorry plight he's in,' said the Congressman. 'Water's
too deep for him to walk ashore, and if he swims, he'll
drag bottom.'

'To the rescue, then,' laughed the Professor. 'Surely
I don't need to explain to you that the people could buy
more stockings with a hundred dollars, if prices were
lower. Well, what is true of stockings is true of goods in
general. Theoretically, then, an increasing volume of
goods could be sold if the price-level fell rapidly enough.'

'Not drowned yet. What next?'

'Next, suppose the price-level remained the same and
people had the same amount of money. Suppose, however, that the money moved around faster, so that each
dollar was spent twice as many times a year as before.
Then the same amount of money would buy twice as

much. That is what I mean by a faster circuit velocity.'

'Plain enough.'

'Very well; that is the second way in which more goods *might* be sold, without an increase in the volume of money. Now the third way I mentioned is increased debts. More stockings could be passed on to consumers, without the passing of more money, if the stockings were sold on instalments or charged on account.'

'Now I get you.'

'But the point is,' continued the Professor, 'that these three ways put together cannot be relied on, in the long run, to move goods as rapidly as the goods can be produced. That point I concede. In fact, every one must concede it, no matter what he may think about the Quantity Theory of Money.'

'All of which means,' said the Business Man, who had been waiting all this time for a good chance to clinch the point, 'that the flow of money to consumers must be increased at the right rate, or the ambition of our Little Gray Man cannot possibly be achieved. And yet — incredible as it may seem — we have no mechanism for bringing about the needed increase.'

'Was not the Federal Reserve System established for that very purpose?' asked the Lawyer.

'No. It was established to provide *producers* with money; and it does that admirably.'

'Do you mean to say' — the Gray Man was incredulous — 'that it is impossible to achieve the one purpose on which I have set my heart, without some agency for bringing about the right flow of money to the people, and yet no agency for that purpose has ever been set up?'

'Exactly that.'

'How is such neglect possible?'

'Because, as the Professor has told us, economic teaching declares that no such agency is needed; since, as long as producers get enough money, consumers automatically get enough.'

'Can we not discuss that assumption now?' asked the Professor.

'Better postpone it a few minutes, I think.'

'Meantime,' said the Professor, 'I must admit that what you have just said uncovers a very neat vein of thought.'

The Professor dug into the vein with all the glee of a prospector, striking gold. He pointed out that unless the flow of money to consumers can be increased, it is folly for any nation to save in the form of additional capital goods, for the only purpose in making such savings is to increase output; but, without an increased flow of money to consumers, the increased output cannot be sold.

'So the savings are wasted,' concluded the Business Man. 'Not wasted in this case, Professor, because the machinery is obsolete, or for any of the other reasons you enumerated, but solely for monetary reasons. It seems to me that you have now gone a long way toward agreement with my whole position.'

'How, then,' the Lawyer asked, 'have we made any progress at all? And we certainly have made progress during the past six or seven years.'

'And at various other times in the past,' said the Business Man. 'But you are all aware that there was nothing like it in the quarter-century before the World War. During that period, in spite of almost incredible gains in industry, gains in real wages in this country did not amount to one half of one per cent a year. Something prevented us from getting very much of our new power and new knowledge into pay envelopes. But I grant you that recently we have done better.'

'Why?' The Lawyer repeated his question as though he had an evasive witness on the stand. 'Why have we done as well as we have done? I hold that it is largely because of low prices and high wages, made possible by reduced unit costs, which in turn are made possible by mass production; and the whole mechanism is kept in motion because the production of goods itself automatically furnishes people with the means of purchase.'

'We shall come to all that presently,' answered the Business Man. 'I am not evading your objections, merely postponing them until I have made my own position clear. According to my theory, we prosper in so far as we approach the right use of our savings. Our failure to use our savings is measured by our idle facilities, both in times of depression and in times of so-called prosperity. It happens that in recent years we have made good use of our savings, and in so doing have brought about a better flow of money to consumers.'

'In what ways?' asked the Lawyer.

'In what ways?' echoed the Professor. 'That is clearly the next question. Your review of the Plain Facts leads you to conclude that progress is possible only in so far as the flow of money to consumers keeps pace with the flow of goods. If the production of goods does not necessarily induce the right flow of money, then I wish you would explain how the right flow has come about in recent years.'

SECTION VIII

'DOESN'T your theory prove too much?' asked the Law-yer. 'If the production of goods does not necessarily yield people enough money to buy the goods, how have people got enough money in recent years?'

'That's it,' echoed the Professor. 'How do you explain the fact that we ever make any progress at all?'

The Business Man was evidently glad to take up that question. 'My first answer,' he said, 'is that sufficient wages are sometimes paid in connection with the con-struction of new capital facilities. I mention only wages; but of course whenever I speak of wages, in this connec-tion, I mean to include salaries, interest, dividends, and all other income that flows to consumers as a part of the process of getting new facilities built.'

The Business Man went on to explain what he meant by that answer: 'Wages,' he pointed out, 'are paid to the workers who build factories, railroads, and machines; to the workers who supply tools and materials; and to those who do the transporting, insuring, financing, and so on. Most of this money is paid to consumers, and most of it is spent by them, before the facilities under construction are ready to supply the markets with goods. So these wages are *advance* payments.'

It was plain that the Business Man attached much

importance to this phase of the subject. 'Especially to be noted,' he said, 'is the fact that these advance payments are made at a time when the only goods for which the wages can be spent are those which have been produced by the old capital facilities.'

Whereupon the Lawyer remarked that he now began to see the point. 'You mean,' said he, 'that these *advance* wages, paid in anticipation of the sale of goods which have not yet been produced, add to the demand for goods without for the time being adding to the supply of goods.'

'Precisely the point,' said the Business Man. 'Such payments, therefore, can sustain consumer demand on a level with output, as long as additional capital facilities are built at the right rate — not too rapidly, not too slowly.'

'And as long,' qualified the Professor, 'as they bring about the needed expansion of the volume of money.'

'Precisely the point again,' agreed the Business Man. 'You seem to be accepting my theory piecemeal.'

'How about capital facilities which are financed out of savings?' asked the Congressman.

'They cannot meet the need for more money, because they do not add to the volume of money. When, for example, a mechanic takes five dollars out of his pay envelope and invests it instead of spending it — invests it in such a way that some other consumer receives and spends the five dollars — there is no increase in money or in consumer demand. So the construction of additional facilities out of *savings* brings about no *additions* to retail buying; and without such additions, as the Professor himself has just pointed out, there is no way in which the actual business world can make use of additional facilities.'

'But the building of facilities actually does involve increases in the volume of money in circulation,' declared the Professor, 'because many of the builders borrow money for the purpose, directly or indirectly, from the banks, and there is a resultant expansion of the volume of bank credit.'

'And therefore an expansion of consumer demand,' added the Business Man. 'Consequently, whenever such construction is at the right rate, it gives business all the driving force that it needs. That is true. In other words, as long as the building of *new* factories, railroads, telephone lines, and so on, brings about a sufficient expansion of money in circulation, the markets for the products of the *old* capital facilities are brisk enough to keep business prosperous. As long as that condition lasts, savings do not cause a shortage of consumer buying. But such construction never long continues in the right volume.'

'And never can,' the Professor asserted. 'I don't see that you are getting anywhere with this analysis.'

'I am stumbling along; that's a fact.' The Business Man smiled, and said again that he wondered how any one could be patient enough to try to follow him at all. 'Still, I think you will find that we are on the way. All I ask you to admit, at this point, is that what I have just been saying ties in snugly with the way we actually do get ahead. First we make progress by creating capital facilities too rapidly. The result is an excess flow of money to consumers, a business boom, and a depression. We cannot have another period of inflation until we are able to use our over-built equipment. That is the real meaning underlying the common saying, "growing up to our capital facilities." When we do catch up, we proceed again to build too rapidly, this time, however, on a larger base. Then we fall back again. So we make fairly good use of our capital equipment savings only in those brief months when we are exceptionally busy accumulating more of such savings than we are able to use. That is the way we have made progress in the past: two steps forward; one step backward; and so on.'

'Now, for the first time,' said the Little Gray Man, 'I understand that expression "growing up to our capital facilities." In view of the immediate needs of so many people, it always seemed to me an outrageously heartless or stupid thing to say.'

'If I see your point,' the Congressman remarked, 'we get on only when the cost of preparing for *future* production is enough, in addition to the cost of *current* production, to give people the money they must have if they are to buy all the goods that are ready. As long as that condition lasts, business is sure to go ahead.'

'Exactly.'

'In other words, we cannot be prosperous to-day unless we are preparing to be prosperous to-morrow. The growth of Kansas proves that. People here in the East could learn a lot from us, if they weren't near-sighted.'

'Trouble is,' said the Salesman, 'you people in the West, too modest. Hide your light under a bushel. Why, that fool cough-drop salesman was tellin' me — Jake — er — er — what the devil *is* his name! Well, anyhow —'

'Anyhow,' interrupted the Congressman, 'the upshot of the matter is?'

'That it is impossible,' declared the Business Man, 'for any country to use the facilities it already has, to a sufficient extent to keep business prosperous, unless it continues to expand bank credit at the right rate in connection with the building of new facilities.'

'I suppose you mean,' reflected the Gray Man, 'that in order to enable the people to buy the output of our present facilities, we have to build new ones; and then, in order that the people may buy the output of the new ones, we have to build more new ones.'

'Exactly, and at the right rate. Don't overlook that.'

'Now I see,' declared the Congressman, 'what you meant when you started all this harangue by saying that we can solve the Little Gray Man's problem only by finding out how to make use of our savings.'

'The idea is new to me,' said the Lawyer.

'New to you!' the Congressman exclaimed. 'Why, man, as far as I can make out, it is new to everybody.'

'But ——,' the Professor began.

'Before you go on,' interrupted the Business Man, 'I want to point out that this is the law of progress which I have been leading up to all the afternoon. I have been hoping, all along, that you would agree to it, once you had agreed to the Plain Facts.'

'But,' objected the Professor, 'economists have *always* insisted that we must save, and invest our savings in improved facilities, in order that we may be better off in the future.'

'In the *future*, yes,' agreed the Congressman. 'Nothing new about that. It is possible to shell corn with the bare hands; but it is easier to use machines, and machines are the result of past savings. Unless somebody, sometime, had used up less than he produced, we should all have to shell corn now and defend ourselves from wild beasts with our bare hands. That, of course, as the Professor says, is old-line economics. It means that we must create better machines to-day in order that we may be better off to-morrow. But it never occurred to me that it is only by getting ready to do better in the *future*, and getting ready at the right rate, that we can do well in the *present*.'

'Nor has that law of progress occurred to economists, as far as I know,' said the Business Man. 'Bear in mind what I said about the Dilemma of Thrift. I pointed out, you recall, that corporate and individual savings, though necessary, cause a deficiency in consumer demand which prevents progress, unless that deficiency is made up in some way.'

Then the Business Man added slowly: 'I wish you could keep that qualification in mind. Savings cause a shortage of consumer buying, *unless the deficiency is made up in some way*. That is as certain as the fact that ten minus one is less than ten; the Ten Minus One Theorem, you might call it — scorned, by the way, or ignored, by most of the professors both here and abroad. I have just pointed out that the deficiency actually is made up at times by an expansion of money, and of wages and other income, at the right rate, in connection with the development of new capital facilities. Yet I have looked through many books on the general principles of economics, without finding any mention of this law of progress.'

'Possibly,' commented the Professor, unable to conceal his impatience, 'because there *is* no such law of progress.'

'If there *is* such a law,' said the Congressman, 'no country can stabilize prosperity. It must either go ahead or fall behind.'

'Or discontinue all savings in the form of increased capital facilities,' added the Lawyer.

'That's a knock-out, Professor,' laughed the Congressman. 'What do you say to that?'

'I suppose I shall have to say,' the Professor answered promptly, 'that you will not find that statement in any economic treatise.'

'At least,' said the Lawyer, 'that theory, if sound, explains why the production of pig-iron is such a good business indicator. I have often asked statistical agencies why, out of a thousand commodities, they pick pig-iron as a forecaster; and the only answer I ever received was that there always has been a close correlation between changes in the demand for pig-iron and changes in general business. Your theory provides an explanation. General business prosperity requires adequate consumer income; that depends on a sufficient expansion of capital facilities; and scarcely any industry can expand without increasing the demand for pig-iron. I must say, Professor, that the further we go, the more convincing this new theory seems to me.'

'But so far,' objected the Professor, 'it is nothing but a theory. What has actually happened during the last decade in the United States which accords with the theory?'

'For one thing, among many, the growth of the automobile industry,' quickly answered the Business Man.

'Without that extraordinary development, I don't see how we could possibly have had such increases in volume of money, in consumer income, in real wages, and in profits. Just think! Within a few years we have developed a new industry which already stands first in volume of output; and we have developed it so successfully that we now turn out seven eighths of the world's output of motor cars — so successfully that our sales of motor cars and motor supplies amounted last year to more than six billion dollars.'

'So successfully,' the Professor added sarcastically, 'that, by easy-payment plans, millions of people have been induced to spend money which they could not afford in buying cars, and time which they could not afford in riding around in them; so successfully that college students have all but lost the use of their legs.'

'Six billions for automobiles!' cried the Gray Man. 'What a loss to makers of shoes, textiles, books ——'

'And hosiery,' interrupted the Salesman. 'Has that been good for business?'

'In reply, answered the Business Man 'let me ask where people would have got those six billion dollars to spend on anything, if it had not been for the automobile? Last year, that industry paid to consumers, directly and indirectly, not far from six billion dollars. In other words, a single industry, non-existent a generation ago, now pays people enough money to enable them to buy the country's total output of bread and, in addition, the total output of woolen, worsted, and silk goods.'

'And most of those six billions,' added the Lawyer, 'actually have been spent, not to buy motor cars, but to buy other things. Every shopkeeper in Detroit knows that. Good for business in general; no doubt.'

'Then,' said the Congressman, 'we do not ride in automobiles because we are prosperous; we are prosperous because we ride in automobiles.'

'But,' urged the Business Man, 'don't overlook the fact that it is the *growth* of the industry which has helped to sustain consumer buying; for a stabilized industry does not make additions to the nation's payroll.'

'And I suppose,' surmised the Lawyer, 'that no other industry ever made such large additions in so short a time. Up to 1907, the year I bought my first car, the capital invested in motor-car production was negligible. Ten years later, it approached a billion dollars; another ten years, and it was around two billions.'

'At least another billion,' added the Business Man, 'we have turned over to consumers in getting ready to supply automobile makers with iron, steel, plate glass, lumber, copper, and paint; two billions more, at least, in connection with oil and tire industries; still other billions in connection with new highways — highways which would not have been built had it not been for the demands and the taxes of car owners.'

'Think, too,' said the Lawyer, 'of the wages paid in constructing garages, filling-stations, office buildings freight cars, and so on, for which the automobile has been partly responsible.'

Then a rambling discussion followed concerning the extent to which the demands of automobile makers have enabled many other industries to go as far as they have gone in borrowing money and enlarging their capital structure.

'But the building industry would have developed, anyway,' objected the Professor.

'Also motion pictures and radios,' added the Salesman.

'And railroads,' said the Congressman. 'Hard to forget them to-day. Telephones, too; steady and amazing growth there.'

'To be sure,' the Business Man agreed. 'No doubt I have exaggerated. Even without the coming of the motor car, there would have been some development in other lines. And as far as such growth brought growth of consumer income, those industries would have helped.'

'They certainly have helped, thanks to the Grand Old Party,' said the Congressman. 'And see the result! The average industrial worker can now buy a car, and ride to work in it every day, and park it in the factory line — if he is lucky enough to find a place — and take his family into the country on Sundays and holidays, and have money enough left to buy fully as much of other things as he could buy before autos were built.'

'And mortgage his future income to do it,' added the Professor, with another sniff of scorn. 'Three fourths of the cars are sold on instalments, and the outstanding debts are fully a billion and a half.'

'True,' assented the Business Man, 'but four million cars a year could not have been sold for cash; and so they would not have been built; and so the country would have been far less prosperous.'

'Nevertheless,' the Lawyer objected, 'I think the rage for instalment buying is demoralizing.'

'But that is beside the point,' contended the Business Man. 'I am not advocating instalment selling; it is no

part of my plan. I am merely answering your question —
the question how we have prospered as well as we have. I
am merely stating the fact that easy-payment sales actually have helped to keep us prosperous, by distributing to
consumers about three billion dollars' worth of automobiles and other goods for which they have not yet paid.
The second point I want to emphasize is still more important: Instalment selling cannot possibly do as much
in the future as it has done in the past, to lift business to
higher levels; for it is the *growth* of instalment selling
which has done the lifting, and a continuation of the past
rate of growth is impossible.'

'Horse sense!' The Congressman continued to voice
his agreement in no uncertain terms. 'So in the future
we must find other means of keeping sales up to output.
In that connection, I have an idea.'

'Release it from solitary confinement!' cried the Salesman.

'My idea is that the chief means, in the past decade,
aside from growth of capital equipment, has been Government expenditures for public works, such as highways,
harbors, canals, parks, and bridges.'

'But,' objected the Lawyer, 'no government can fill the
people's pockets by taking money away from them as
taxes and giving it back to them as wages. That is like
trying to lengthen a blanket by cutting a piece off the top
and sewing it on the bottom.'

'Nevertheless,' answered the Business Man, 'the
Member from Kansas is right; for when governments
finance public works by loans which involve expansion

of bank credit, as is often the case, they *do* add to consumer income. Government bonds, for example, are
often used by the owners as collateral for bank loans.
Again, whenever the necessity of paying taxes forces men
to borrow money from banks, the result may be an expansion of bank credit, even though the borrowers pay
their taxes out of cash on hand, and are then forced to
borrow money for other uses.'

'That,' the Professor admitted, 'is an important fact
which is often overlooked. And I must say that you are
digging deeper than I gave you credit for.'

'Note, also, this other important point,' continued the
Business Man. 'Governments thus add to consumer income, without adding to the goods which consumers are
expected to buy. So public expenditures of that kind
surely do help business, whenever consumer demand is
inadequate.'

'Such expenditures certainly have been large in recent
years,' said the Professor. 'Federal, State, and local taxes
combined are now over eight billion dollars, and that is
nearly four times the highest pre-War total — two and a
half times, even with allowance for change in the purchasing power of the dollar. Back in 1913 Government expenditures, Federal, State, and local, were not nine per
cent of the total national income; now they are at least
fourteen per cent. That means that one dollar out of
every seven is spent for public purposes.'

'And that means,' the Gray Man added, 'that public
expenditures are now nearly half as large as all the wages
paid in all the manufacturing plants of the entire country.'

'But you cannot blame the Federal Government for

that.' The Congressman did not have to consult his pocket files on this point. 'State taxes have increased fully one hundred per cent since 1919, and local taxes more than fifty per cent, while Federal taxes have actually *decreased* about forty per cent. State and local taxes are now about sixty per cent of the total.'

'The total tax, however,' explained the Business Man, 'is not our main interest, as far as consumer income is concerned. For when, as was the case last year, State and local governments collect only five billions in taxes and spend about seven billions, a large amount of money which is spent on highways, waterworks, public buildings, and the like, must come, not from taxes, but from loans. Now, as I just pointed out, many of these loans, directly or indirectly, involve an expansion of the volume of money in circulation and are therefore a gain on the consumer side.'

'So the people get more money with which to buy things,' said the Gray Man, 'without in the process turning out more things which they are expected to buy.'

'Exactly. There is an increase in demand, but no increase in supply.'

'Still,' the Lawyer objected, 'it is bad public policy for governments to go ahead spending money at such a rate.'

'Perhaps so,' answered the Business Man, 'but that is beside the point. I am no more advocating an increase of Government expenditures, than a moment ago I was advocating an increase of instalment buying. I am still merely answering your question. Whether or not the large increases in public expenditures in recent years have been desirable, the fact remains that they have added largely to the income of consumers, and thus have helped business to prosper.'

'But' — the Lawyer, true to his profession, was still offering objections — 'public expenditures cannot long increase at the rate of the past ten years, for at that rate all the money the people get would presently be demanded as taxes.'

'Consequently,' concluded the Business Man, 'we now face this issue: Since we cannot long increase either instalment selling or public expenditures, at the rate which we have maintained in the recent past, we must provide for the right flow of money in some other way, or suffer a serious recession of business.'

'I must say,' conceded the Lawyer, 'that I see no escape from that conclusion. In fact, even with the help of these huge increases in public spending, and even with more than three billion dollars' worth of goods sold on instalments which are not yet paid for, and even with the stimulus of the growth of the automobile and building industries, there has not been enough buying to sustain the wholesale commodity price-level. What would have happened without these extraordinary aids to business?'

'Hard times; just what they have had in England and many other countries,' the Business Man answered. 'Now, still further to answer your question, let me remind you that we have disposed of a large volume of our increased output by sending it abroad to people who cannot pay for it. But that is another means of stimulating business which cannot go on indefinitely, at least with any benefits to our own people.'

'No question about the facts,' commented the Lawyer. 'Since 1914, our merchandise exports have ex-
ceeded imports by more than twenty-two billion dollars
— an amount ten times the capitalization of our automobile industry.'

'That whole situation is absurd!' exclaimed the Congressman. 'Our foreign debtors cannot pay their debts
to us except with goods; we have not made it possible for
them to pay us with goods; yet, by arranging new loans,
we are constantly increasing their debts, without having
any idea how they will be able to pay what they already
owe. Any corner grocer in Kansas who did business that
way would have to have his head examined.'

'It is certainly crazy,' the Professor asserted. 'All due
to indefensible protective tariffs, patched together by
your Grand Old Party. I suppose the ——'

'Not so indefensible as you may think, under conditions as they are,' said the Business Man. 'But, for the
moment, I am neither defending nor condemning our
foreign-trade policy. I am still answering your question.
I am pointing out that one way in which we have con-
trived to keep on producing and disposing of our so-
called "surplus" goods — goods in excess of what our
own people can buy and pay for — is by sending the
goods to people abroad who cannot pay for them.'

'Only a temporary expedient,' remarked the Congressman.

'That's just my point. There is but one permanent
solution of the problem; and that is to enable the people
of the United States to buy, and pay for, as much as they
can produce of consumers' goods, or the full equivalent in
the products of other countries.'

'Again,' declared the Lawyer, 'I must say that this approach to the subject is entirely new to me. It is certainly radically different in parts from the only economics I ever learned; and I am not yet fully prepared to accept it. I have a feeling that there may be something wrong with it; but I admit I cannot put my finger on the weak spot.'

'I think I can locate it, when my time comes,' asserted the Professor, confidently.

'Perhaps,' the Lawyer suggested, 'it has to do with the influence of gold production. That was always one of the fundamentals of the old economics; but you have not mentioned it once to-day.'

'Of course that should be taken into account,' said the Business Man. 'If the production of gold could be relied on to provide consumers with enough money to buy the output of industry, there could be no general overproduction, and so no point to our discussion. What are the facts, Professor?'

'The facts are clear enough, and on this point you happen to be right. The volume of gold production does not adjust itself promptly to the monetary needs of business; and there is no reason why it should.'

'I can see for the first time,' the Lawyer observed, 'how such prosperity as we have had in recent years must have come about. It must have resulted largely from wages paid in connection with new capital facilities and new public works — aided by a favorable balance of trade and, I am forced to admit, by the growth of instalment selling, all of which has brought about an increase of consumer income. This must have been just about enough to enable us to use our facilities to the extent that we have used them, but not enough to enable us to use them at any approach to capacity.'

'Right,' said the Business Man. 'But don't overlook the fact that even such partial success has come largely by chance. There has been no adequate organized effort to bring it about, or to measure what was needed to bring it about. Nor has ——'

'Even so,' interposed the Lawyer, 'the result has been real progress.'

'In the United States, yes; but in most other countries, no. As a matter of fact, additions to consumer income which grow out of the construction of new capital facilities and public works and the mining of gold, are almost certain to be more than enough or less than enough to keep business going forward on an even keel. There is nothing in ordinary business financing which automatically brings about the right adjustment. That fact creates a crucial problem. The first need is the discovery that there *is* such a problem. The next need is a plan for dealing with the problem.'

'And your own plan?' asked the Lawyer. 'Are you ready to outline that now?'

'Yes, ready and willing.'

SECTION IX

THE Business Man's traveling class in economics, each with his characteristic frame of mind, settled down to listen to the proposed programme. Superficial, the Professor naturally expected it to be; probably a fiat money scheme, or some other measure in violation of sound principles of economics. What was new in the plan, he felt sure, would not be true; and what was true, would not be new. So he puffed away at his pipe in contentment, confident that, when his time came, he could expose the fallacies in the Business Man's argument. The Lawyer, still kindly in his attitude, but equally skeptical, was already beginning to classify and brief all the objections he could think of to taking any action at all. The Congressman, on the other hand, hoped and expected to hear some programme which could be made effective through legislation. The Salesman, tired of theorizing, was also eager to hear some plan for action. Most eager and confident of all, needless to say, was the Little Gray Man. With a thrill which vibrated in his voice, he remarked that at last he felt well on the way toward much that he had long been seeking.

'In explaining the Proposed Policy,' the Business Man began, 'I sometimes find it helpful to use the Federal Reserve System to illustrate what I want to accomplish.

Luckily, we have a bank director with us, and I am going to ask him to tell us what change the Federal Reserve System has brought about in the money market.'

'Well,' replied the Lawyer, wondering what this had to do with the subject, 'formerly, as you know, banks had to demand payment of many loans in time to meet the periodic shortage of money at the season of crop movements; but the very fact that banks thus anticipated a disturbance in the money market, helped to create the disturbance. Under the Federal Reserve System, on the other hand, the very fact that banks know that there is not going to be any serious disturbance, prompts them to use their money in such a way as not to cause a disturbance.'

'And a slight rise in money rates, when it does come, how much does that disturb business?'

'Hardly at all,' answered the Lawyer. 'Under the old banking system, as you well remember, even a slight rise in money rates sometimes drove men to act as though they were certain of a further rise, which of course helped to cause a further rise.'

'And now?'

'Now, as you have observed, a rise in rates hardly bothers business men at all, for they are confident that the Federal Reserve System will help to prevent a further rise.'

'Exactly,' said the Business Man, 'and nothing could better illustrate my main point. At present there is no agency which does for business in general what the Federal Reserve System does for the money market. Now I propose the setting-up of an agency which shall take the leadership in bringing about measures to stop that rising spiral of business inflation of which we spoke at the outset, as soon as it gets started; and equally prompt measures to stop the falling spiral of deflation, once that gets started.'

'To show exactly what you mean by that analogy,' suggested the Congressman, 'I wish you would start at the beginning and outline your whole plan, as briefly as possible.'

'Just what I wanted you to do some time ago,' said the Professor.

'But I could not do that,' the Business Man explained, 'until I had brought before you the Plain Facts on which the Plan is based. Why that is so will become clear as we proceed.'

'Now we're off!' exclaimed the Congressman. Then, patting the Professor on the back, he added, 'And we'll all hold back our objections until the whole plan is outlined.'

'To begin with,' said the Business Man, 'we have already agreed, as I understand it, that there is no possibility of attaining what our Gray Man so ardently desires — full employment, higher real wages, better standards of living for the workers — unless industry can continue to sell an increased output of goods. But that is impossible unless the money income of consumers is such that they actually buy the increased output. The income which they receive from producers of goods does not enable them to buy the increased output; for, as I have already reminded you, no successful producer pays out, in putting goods on the market, as much money as he receives from consumers for the goods.'

'Looks like the law of diminishing returns,' said the Congressman.

'Never heard of it. When was that law passed, Old Solon?' asked the Salesman.

'Forget technical terms.' The Business Man, eager to outline the Plan before the men were tired out, was trying to prevent the discussion from wandering. 'You all know what I mean. Just remember that a profitable selling price is higher than costs.'

'In other words,' threw in the Salesman, 'business is business.'

'And remember, furthermore,' added the Business Man, 'that consumers do not spend even as much money as they receive; for in the aggregate, they constantly increase their savings, and ought to do so. Consequently, if consumers are to continue to do enough buying to sustain prosperity, they must receive the needed balance of income from other sources. These facts, I take it, are all self-evident. Moreover ——'

'By no means self-evident,' interrupted the Professor; 'but go ahead with your outline.'

'Well, then, I have just pointed out that the construction of additional capital facilities and public works sometimes does enable consumers to obtain the needed balance of money. That money is partly their own invested savings, flowing back to them, and partly new money which has been created by the expansion of bank credit. You have already agreed, Professor, that we must have a constantly increasing volume of money, if we are to make progress?'

'With that I fully agree.'

'Now, if the money which flows to consumers from all these sources is such that they buy nearly the total output of consumers' goods — some at a profit to producers, some at a loss, but on the whole at prices which sustain business as a whole — the savings which have been invested in capital facilities, both old and new, can be used to the best advantage. Otherwise, it is not possible.'

'And again,' interposed the Lawyer, 'that is what you meant at the outset, when you said that we could make progress only by making the right use of our savings.'

'Exactly,' said the Business Man. 'Note, however, this crucial point: the income which consumers receive from these two sources — creation of capital facilities and public works — is sure to be either more than enough or less than enough to meet the needs.'

'Necessarily so?' the Lawyer asked.

'Necessarily, as things now go; for in any given period, the men who determine how much money is paid out in new construction are by no means the same men as those who determine the flow of goods into consumers' markets. And neither group — mark this second crucial point — neither group knows just how much the other group is doing. Neither group, therefore, has any means of *even knowing* what it should do to help the general situation.'

'In other words,' commented the Congressman, 'the trouble is this: Nobody knows how much money consumers need in order to buy the current output at prices which keep business going steadily forward; nobody knows how far short of what they need is the part furnished by producers of goods; and so, of course, nobody knows how much money consumers should receive in connection with the creation of capital facilities and public works. I agree with you that, under these conditions, consumers are sure to receive either too much money, or too little money, to keep business going steadily forward.'

'Now, if consumers receive too much,' the Business Man went on, 'prices rise, speculation increases, and business rushes forward toward a boom and collapse. The movement does not correct itself; on the contrary, there is what the Professor has called a vicious spiral of inflation. If, on the other hand, consumers receive too little income, prices fall, production is reduced, men are thrown out of work, and business depression ensues. Here, again, the movement goes from bad to worse; there is a vicious spiral of *de*flation. And so, as I said at the outset, there is no chance that adequate corrective influences will long be brought to bear if we continue, as at present, to rely on individual initiative; for no individual either knows when to act, or has any responsibility for acting.'

'Right again,' said the Congressman. 'And so collective leadership is necessary.'

'Under such leadership,' continued the Business Man, 'we must first of all find out when to act. We can do that by measuring, more accurately than ever before, changes in the price-level of consumers' goods, changes in unemployment and in various other factors. These indexes will show when it is the right time to increase, when the right time to decrease, expenditures for capital facilities and public works. In the past, we have never known until too late. But as soon as we have a guide, we can take timely steps toward bringing about the right flow of money to consumers. If the flow is too much, we can reduce it; if too little, we can increase it.'

'Why not?' In his eagerness the Gray Man forgot his intention to leave the floor to the other men. 'How stupid,' he exclaimed, 'to stand helplessly by when inflation begins to carry us on toward a collapse, or when a depression begins! We do not resign ourselves that way to periodic floods and drought, however natural they may be. We build dams; hold back the water when there is too much; release it when more is needed. We do not say it is useless to interfere with the laws of Nature.'

'Stupid is the word' — the Congressman spoke with conviction — 'for it is easier to control floods of money than floods of water; easier to supply a deficiency of credit than a deficiency of rainfall.'

'In substance,' the Lawyer remarked, 'the Plan seems to be, first, to measure the forces which make us prosperous while we are prosperous, particularly the right flow of consumer income; and, second, to do whatever is necessary to sustain that flow.'

'That sums it up in general terms,' said the Business Man. 'Under such a policy, savings can be used to the utmost advantage, and production can be steadily increased, without the serious checks caused by inflation and deflation. The result will be less unemployment and more real wages. Thus the benefits will be enjoyed most largely by those who are now in greatest need.'

'That, then, is your Proposed Policy?' the Professor asked.

'Yes, in substance. I do not offer it as an adequate statement.'

'You don't!' exclaimed the Congressman. 'Well, it's enough to convince me. Far-reaching, I call it, and yet practical. I can see at once that it throws light on all sorts of measures which I have always had to vote on in the dark.'

But the Kindly Lawyer was frankly skeptical. 'Your analysis is of the utmost importance, if true,' he admitted. 'Indeed, if you can prove your case, you can show that no end of current economic notions are incompetent, immaterial, and irrelevant. But it is hard for me to believe that such a pregnant economic analysis, if really sound, would not have been acted on long ago.'

'Seems sound to me,' declared the Congressman. 'A Business Man's Theory of Economics. That's what it is. Just what I have long needed.'

'I still hold that your theory is too simple, far too simple,' the Professor asserted, punctuating his objection, however, with a less contemptuous rabbit-like sniff than formerly. 'Our highly complicated financial and industrial mechanism works best when left alone.'

'But,' retorted the Business Man, 'when individuals are left alone, as at present, to act in the dark, consider what happens. The decisions of certain men, as I have said, determine what quantity of goods is made and sent to market. Isn't it true that, meantime, the decisions of other men — men who determine the volume of new construction, public and private — largely determine whether consumers get enough money to take those very goods off the market? How, then, is any one to know what balance of income it is necessary for consumers to have?'

The Professor knitted his brows. Noticing his perplexity, the Business Man added: 'Perhaps an illustration will show what I mean. Suppose, in order to build a highway along the Hudson River, the State of New York appropriates a part of the funds. Suppose the Federal Government undertakes to furnish the necessary balance. But suppose the Government has no means of knowing what the road will cost or how much the State will pay. What chance, then, has the Government of furnishing exactly the right balance, when it knows neither the total amount of money needed to construct the highway, nor the proportion which the State of New York will provide? Now that, in general, is the business situation to-day.'

'As I understand it,' said the Lawyer, 'you propose, by collective leadership, to enable the people to receive just enough income to enable them to keep on saving, and yet to buy the output of goods which are retained for use at home, and the full equivalent, in imports, of all the goods which are exported.'

'Substantially that.'

'Do you mean without a change in the price-level?' asked the Professor.

'Yes, let us make that assumption for the present.'

'Can we not make progress, even when prices are falling, provided the fall is due to lower unit costs of production?'

'Yes, under certain conditions,' answered the Business Man. 'For the present, all I want to make clear is that the Policy I propose is just as important under those conditions as under any other conditions. No matter what decline in prices may be possible, due to lower unit costs, the right flow of money to consumers is still essential. But in the past, even when unit costs were falling, we have never known, until too late, whether the flow of money was too slow or too rapid; and therefore at no time have we had a guide to tell us what to do.'

'I understand, then,' said the Gray Man, 'that you propose to find out how to sustain the forces which make us prosperous while we are prosperous.'

'That's it,' the Business Man assented. 'In other words, we should measure with greater precision than ever before the forces which bring about good times, and take whatever steps are necessary to keep those forces in operation.'

'And they cannot operate,' contributed the Lawyer, 'unless there is the right increase of consumer income. We all agree with you on that point. But those who are familiar with economic theory tell me that economists have long held that the very process of producing the additional output yields people just about enough money to buy it.'

'I am aware that many economists have long held that to be true,' quickly countered the Business Man, with a quizzical look in his eyes, 'but it happens to be false. It is not in accord with the facts of business.'

Whereupon the Semi-Silk Salesman was heard to remark, 'It ain't what a man don't know that makes him

a fool; it's the awful sight of things he knows that ain't
so.'

Even the Professor smiled; but the Little Gray Man,
intent on his purpose, urged the Business Man to go on.
'Why,' he asked, 'has nothing ever been done, on the
basis of your theory, to bring about the right flow of
money to consumers?'

'Apparently,' answered the Business Man, 'because of
the assumption at the very foundation of traditional economic theory, which the Lawyer just referred to; the
assumption that there is no such problem as I have outlined, because production automatically provides consumers with the means of purchase. As I understand it,
Professor, that is the point you have been impatiently
waiting to discuss. And now I am ready for you. But
I suppose we ought to give the other men a chance to
escape. You know, we haven't yet heard the story of the
blind beggar.'

The Gray Man said that, for all he cared, the blind
beggar could wait his turn till Judgment Day. He himself was a blind beggar, he said, begging for light on the
great economic riddle; and, although he was convinced
that the Business Man was right, he was nevertheless
ready to bestow a blessing on any one who would drop
some more Plain Facts into his tin cup.

'Go ahead,' urged the Congressman. 'And take my
word, what you have said so far is good stuff. It all
squares with everything I know about business.'

'Straight goods, one hundred per cent silk,' assented
the Salesman. 'Nothin' but everyday business. When
does the economics come in?'

'Plain Facts, sure enough,' the Gray Man added. 'Why has nothing been done on the basis of those Facts? I can't understand it. If the reason is this fundamental assumption, which the Professor calls true and the Business Man calls false, then I, for one, am eager to hear them clash on that issue.'

'Very well,' consented the Business Man. 'But here we are almost in the station, with ten minutes to wait. What do you say to a little air and exercise?'

'A good idea,' said the Gray Man, as they all prepared to leave the car. 'But don't give us the slip. You have just reached the crux of your disagreement with the Professor, whom you have put off all this time. You owe it to all of us to go on with the fray.'

SECTION X

'To build upon solid ground: that is all the Business Man
would have us do.' The Little Gray Man kept saying that to himself, as he walked up and down the platform.

Here was a proposal to start with human beings as they
are; to preserve all that is essential in the established order; to reject nothing except theories which are discredited by everyday experience. The Business Man was not
proposing to enrich the poor by despoiling the wealthy;
or to abolish private ownership of land; or to print
money as the Russians had done; or to substitute untried
motives for the present mainsprings of industrial life. On
the contrary, he was urging the necessity of doing very
much what is being done to-day, but doing it all intelligently, on the basis of measurements, directed by a principle which is now lacking. Guided by that principle,
he would have men save in the future in such a way that
their savings could be used to advantage.

The Gray Man thought of that group: the conservative Lawyer, the cautious Professor, the keen Congressman, the practical Salesman, led by the successful Business Man. Here were men who, among them, knew the
facts; men who saw what was going on every day — in
fields, mines, factories, banks, markets, legislatures, law

courts; men who knew the realities and accepted them. Certainly such men would not support policies which required changing the nature of markets or the nature of men. Surely, the Gray Man said to himself, if such representative leaders of thought and action can be induced to set themselves to the task, they can work out something sound, effective; something which will commend itself at once to the judgment of men everywhere.

As much could not be said of any of the other far-reaching programmes which the Gray Man had considered from time to time. There was the Red-Haired Orator, for example. That destroyer had no idea what the forces were which had achieved gains for the workers in the past; no thought of strengthening and using those forces in the future. Kill them and begin over! That was his programme. Nor had he any conception of the hard and intelligent work which the hated capitalists had performed in the past, to the great benefit of mankind; no intention of trying to make these capitalists work harder and more intelligently in the future for the still greater benefit of mankind. 'Destroy the bloodsuckers.' That was his one idea. In short, this dynamiter was out to blow up the whole established system of production and exchange — a highly intricate mechanism, of the workings of which he was profoundly ignorant — to overthrow the system, together with whatever intelligence and devotion could be found at the head of it. And in its place, what?

The Red-Haired Orator did not know.

He was typical in that respect, as the Gray Man could

now see more clearly than ever, of the many reformers who, at various times in the past, had half-won his allegiance. He had no objections to their programmes, not even to that of the Red-Haired Orator, except that they would not work — would leave Joe Burns just as insecure, just as anxious, just as bewildered as ever. And it was the Gray Man's overpowering urge to make the world a better place for such men as Joe. That was the passion which had impelled him toward socialism and every other 'ism' which promised to open up the Road to Plenty. It was his clearness of mind, on the other hand, which had kept him from plunging into one futile reform after another.

Now, at last, both his feelings and his thoughts were urging him in the same direction. He was entirely satisfied with the Business Man's programme and eager for action, though he understood why the Professor and the Lawyer, by virtue of their callings, would first insist on offering further objections.

The hope which had lifted the Little Gray Man out of his unhappiness, early in the day, had now become complete confidence in the Business Man. Here was the first person he had met, among those who had anything to offer toward solving the problems of poverty and enforced idleness, who seemed to know much about the actual business world. Here, moreover, was a man with powers of leadership. There was something inspiring about ——

About what? The Gray Man stopped, and looked closely at the Business Man as he walked down the platform. About his eyes, perhaps, his bearing, his voice.

Or was it that his certainty of what might be done grew out of his daily dealing with hard facts? Anyway, the Business Man inspired confidence. What might he not accomplish, if only he had sufficient urge!

The Little Gray Man thought of the families he had just visited in Linton, struggling on the verge of destitution, and the feeble old men in the wood-yard, forcing their rheumatic joints to do enough work to keep them out of the Poor House. He thought of those girls in the South End who had sought in vain, week after week, for decent means of support. Then he remembered his futile attempt, on the station platform, to think of something both cheerful and honest to say to discouraged Joe Burns. To do something permanently good, something more than occasional charity for such as these — to help to remove at least some of the economic causes of their misery — had long been the Gray Man's dominant passion. And now ——

Could it be that these exciting hopes were born of nothing but his own eagerness? Would this turn out to be merely another personally conducted tour through realms of theory; another round trip which would leave all the travelers exactly where they started? No, the Gray Man could not believe that. Still, it was disquieting to have the discussion go on and on, with no more suggestion of action than as though it were a game of chess.

What could be done about it all — done right away? That was the one question the Gray Man wanted to ask, as soon as the discussion was resumed. It was all interesting — this theorizing. No doubt it was true that nothing could be done in a large way for Joe Burns and millions of other industrial cast-offs, unless ways could be found of developing capital goods and public works at the right rate. What of it? The Gray Man wanted to know precisely what measures could be found.

That question the Gray Man was determined to ask, and keep on asking. His fellow-travelers had called him a Thorn in the Flesh. Very well, he would prick the sides of their intent, if they had any. If they had none, he might supply one. His own immediate intent was to prevent this riot of talk from ending in talk.

'Still at it, I see. So concerned over old Joe Burns that you almost ran into me.' The Congressman looked down on him with his engaging smile. Then, taking the Gray Man's arm, he said: 'Come and walk with me. Fact is, I like you, like the cut of your jib, like the direct way you go at things, like your impatience with all this hair-splitting theorizing. You ought to go West. Take my word, you would make good from the start, out where I live. But that learned Professor, with his academic circumflex, and his failure to see the main idea while pursuing endless qualifications, and his caution about committing himself to anything, and his damned patronizing tolerance of men who have forgotten more about business than he ever knew — he almost gets my goat!'

'You sound fierce; but you couldn't frighten anybody with that twinkle in your eye.'

'Twinkle or no twinkle, I'd like to see somebody take a fall out of that Professor. I was in business twenty years, before the voters arose as one man and demanded that I save the country; but I have never found a professor who would admit that I know anything about business.

'Take my word ——'

'Take *my* word,' broke in the Gray Man, 'we shall *need* the Professor before we get through. I have a hunch that he will show the Business Man some neglected points; show him that these hair-splitting economists can help build his own case. If the Professor ever gets a chance, I expect him to restate the Policy, and qualify it, and define its terms, so that the professors themselves can support it. But first he will insist that too much is claimed for the Policy. Even I can see that. I haven't said so, because I've been thrilled to find a business man who has *any* plan for action. But as for abolishing poverty — Gr-e-a-t Jupiter! I've seen enough to know that nothing will reach *all* the causes. Still, there are far-reaching causes which *can* be reached.'

'Right you are!'

'And the Professor can help us. Come now,' — the Gray Man put his hand on the broad shoulder of the Congressman — 'admit that he is really a very good fellow, even though he does pursue the truth, in every nook and corner, more relentlessly than you and the Business Man do.'

'Oh, I suppose so, except for his occupational disease. Painters have painters' colic, plumbers have lead poisoning, and professors have the academic mind.'

'And congressmen?'

'We have infantile paralysis. Makes it hard for us to get anywhere.'

'But what is it that makes you scorn professors, and then give so much weight to their ideas?'

'Now you've said it, my Little Gray Man. Take my word, Congress will never adopt any far-reaching measures of the kind you want, without hearing from the professors.'

'So we need their help,' said the Gray Man, 'and you are just the man to get it, just the man to cure this Professor of his academic inertia, and your friend, the Lawyer, of his "nothing can be done about it" infection. That's *his* occupational disease. Here is a chance for you to fire this enterprise with the spirit of the West.'

'Fact is,' said the Congressman, 'I'm getting more and more fired myself. The more I hear about the Business Man's Theory, the more hopeful I am that it may be the unifying principle which I've long been looking for. Here I've fooled around, session after session, dealing with taxes, tariffs, public debts, soldiers' bonuses, appropriations for public works, pay of Government employees, and the like, and feeling all the time that I didn't know half what I needed to know about the effects of all such measures on general prosperity. Why should Congress appropriate even a million dollars for anything, without giving a thought to the trend of prices at the time, the volume of unemployment, and so on? Yet I have seen bills carrying a hundred million dollars passed without the slightest consideration —— But here I am making a speech, and the train is starting.'

'Applause,' cried the Gray Man. 'Write that into the *Record*.' And, as they boarded the train, he added: 'We want an extension of those remarks in the next session of the Smoking-Room Congress. But we must have more than remarks. They are not legal tender in Kansas; they don't pay off farm mortgages. And remember, it won't do Joe Burns any good for us to find out how to construct the Road to Plenty, if we don't begin to build it until he has died of worry.'

SECTION XI

As soon as the six men were again seated in the smoking-room, the Professor, keen for the fray, said to the Business Man, 'Are you ready now to hear my objection to your theory?'

'Ready and eager.'

'First of all, then, let me concede that the rate of progress which is inherently possible, is *not* possible unless the flow of money to consumers increases about as rapidly as the flow of consumers' goods. Such an increase of income — I concede this point, too — cannot be maintained unless the investment of *new* money in productive enterprise grows at an increasing rate, and continues to grow at an increasing rate. But perfectly steady growth, free from setbacks, is impossible, since the causes of industrial fluctuations are partly random, sporadic, and unforeseeable. You, on your part, will surely concede that point.'

'Certainly. Minor setbacks, of short duration, are inevitable.'

'Now, my next point is that the financial processes which determine growth are largely self-regulating. The production of goods, considered as a whole, automatically yields consumers the money wherewith to buy the goods, in such a way that the processes of production and exchange, when left alone as in the past, induce about as steady and rapid progress as it is possible to attain by any monetary measures. That, as I understand it, is the point you do not concede.'

'Yes, precisely the point,' rejoined the Business Man incisively. 'And that is the main issue on which we clash. You and the Lawyer, with your analytic minds, have seen from the beginning that my argument must stand or fall on that issue. Now you see why I have kept putting you off. I wanted to prepare the way. I also wanted to make it clear to all of you that this Automatic Production-Consumption Theory really *is* the crux of our conflict.'

Then, turning to the Little Gray Man, he added, 'Incidentally, in what I have to say about that Automatic Theory, I shall give my answer to your own question: Why has nothing ever been done, on the basis of the Plain Facts, to bring about the right flow of money?'

'Now, then,' exclaimed the Congressman, 'we are ready for the fray!'

'Bully!' cried the Semi-Silk Salesman. 'I will referee the bout. Ring the bell.'

'A fight without gloves,' the Business Man said earnestly, again standing up in his excitement. 'That's what the issue calls for. The truth is, my feelings are too intense for me to try to soften the blows.'

'I am not a principal in this fight,' said the Lawyer, 'but I am sitting in the Professor's corner, and I should like to say that the Professor's point is just the one I made awhile ago. It seems to me that in order to get at the bottom of the whole matter, we must dig beneath the money surface of things. We must realize that trade is, after all, nothing but barter, since the final outcome is always the exchange of goods against goods. Consequently, all the goods in existence constitute, not only the total supply of goods, but also the total demand for goods; so in the long run supply and demand can never be anything but equal.'

'As the same theory is often stated,' the Business Man observed, 'all the goods in existence are owned by somebody — that we have to admit — so somebody must always have the wherewithal to buy those goods. It follows that each addition to supply creates an exactly equivalent addition to demand. So production itself takes care of consumption. Is that what you mean?'

'Substantially that,' the Lawyer replied. 'Only the other day I was talking with an able client of mine, himself a business man, and he remarked that people who are always wanting to do something to make consumer income keep pace with the output of goods, completely overlook the fact that production itself furnishes the means of purchase.'

'I see,' observed the Congressman. 'It is a sleight-of-hand performance. The process of making a five-dollar hat is supposed to draw forth from the hat and place in somebody's pocket — presto! with the magician's sleeves rolled up — a five-dollar bill with which to buy the hat.'

'That's about it,' the Business Man agreed.

'That's not it at all,' replied the Professor. 'You are setting up a straw argument, which it is child's play to demolish. Nobody contends that every article, or even every industry, yields consumers the right amount of money. The classical argument has to do only with production as a whole. Now, may I suggest that before we come to blows, we try something novel in the way of fights? Why not see if we can find out exactly what we are fighting about?'

'An' spoil the fight!' The Referee-Salesman, afraid of losing his job, remarked that this must be one of those pacifist professors.

'Even at the risk of spoiling the fight, let me give you the traditional statement of that Automatic Production-Consumption Theory.'

The Professor, now plainly aroused, knocked the ashes out of his pipe with more than usual vigor, took off his horn-rimmed spectacles, rubbed them hard, put them on again, and began: 'According to the generally accepted theory, the processes of production, *in the long run*, cause or involve the distribution of money, sufficient in amount to pay for the goods produced by those processes. I include, of course, all payments of money which are made in connection with setting up the instruments for producing the goods in question. This theory does not hold, mind you, that the processes of production provide the means of purchasing goods at the *maximum* rate at which goods conceivably might be produced in some Utopian society where no plant or producer was ever idle. The traditional theory asserts nothing more than this: that production itself yields consumers an amount of money which, on the average and in the long run, is enough to enable consumers to purchase nearly all the goods which are actually produced; and at prices which maintain production indefinitely, without permanent diminution in its average rate; in fact, as experience shows, with increases in the rate of production, when averaged over long periods. And that happens, generation after generation, in spite of frequent, temporary setbacks. In other words, the process of the distribution of goods through the medium of money *does* work automatically. Virtually all the goods which are turned out *do* get sold at some price; that is as plain a fact as any in your own list.'

'In short,' concluded the Lawyer, 'production *does* increase; distribution automatically and inevitably follows production; from which unquestioned facts it is perfectly logical to conclude, as John Stuart Mill did conclude, that the industrial and financial world need be concerned only with problems of production.'

'And don't overlook the fact,' added the Professor, 'that the goods which actually *do* get sold, through this automatic process, show per capita, secular, progressive increases — very gratifying gains, in the long view — cause enough for optimism.'

'Cause for optimism!' the Business Man exclaimed. 'Cause for optimism, when the net result for great masses of people is the conditions which our Gray Man has so vividly set before us — want and anxiety which call to High Heaven for relief! To be sure, mankind *has* made some progress. But why must it be so slow? That is the question we have been discussing all day. And one answer to that question — not the only answer, by any means, but an important answer — is the very fact that the Powers-That-Be have regarded this long-run Automatic Theory as a justification of things as they are. Focusing their attention mainly on goods and on long periods of time, they have neglected short-term, monetary aspects of production and consumption, and thus have missed the chief clue to the problem. For in any short period — say, one year or two years — the money which is distributed in the productive processes does *not* automatically finance the sale of the output. And what happens in one or two years may be enough to cause a depression of business. It is, in fact, these repeated, *temporary* breakdowns of production which prevent the *long-run* progress which otherwise would be possible. And it is precisely because the productive processes, everything included, can*not* be relied on, in any short period, to furnish people the right amount of money, that production periodically *does* break down. It does not matter how much money consumers may have received in a previous period of time, or how much they may receive in some future period of time. That is largely beside the point. The extent to which business uses its productive capacity *this* year depends mainly on the money consumers receive this year.'

'That's it,' agreed the Congressman. 'In deciding how much to produce, nobody asks what happens *in the long run*. What happened last year, last month? What is likely to happen next year, next month? Those are the practical questions. In the long run, all the water in the rivers of Vermont finds its way to the sea. What of it? That plain fact doesn't help any one to decide whether to prepare *this* year for a flood or a drought.'

'And so,' concluded the Business Man, 'it is impossible to find out why we have these periodic depressions, and why, partly in consequence of these depressions, we produce far less than we are equipped to produce over long periods of time, unless we find out exactly why, in short periods, production fails to finance consumption. The old long-term theory either explicitly declared that there was no such problem or ignored it. In either case, that theory was one of the stumbling blocks to progress.'

'Don't think for a moment that I shall deny all that,' said the Professor, earnestly. 'In your enthusiasm, no doubt you have overstated the case. That is natural. But I admit at once that what you have just said, when properly qualified, merits more study than it has yet received.'

The Business Man's face lighted up in appreciation of even that small measure of agreement.

Then, turning to the Professor and the Lawyer, he said: 'You have already paid your respects to business men. You have said they are superficial, unversed in economic theory, bound to rule-of-thumb procedure, and always going pell-mell like a flock of sheep in the wrong direction. Well, there is much ground for your criticism. Now, having admitted that, let me direct a few blows, straight from the shoulder, at the economists of the past.'

With deep feeling the Business Man proceeded:

'For more than a century, orthodox economists, dominant in the universities, prescribers of the only system of economics that most men ever studied, have been absolutely and inexcusably wrong on this crucial issue. First they assumed, merely assumed, mind you' — warming up to his subject, he began to try to pace the narrow floor — 'almost incredible, what I am telling you, but the exact truth — these lords of the domain of economic theory merely assumed, without even an attempt at proof, that the financing of production itself provides people with the means of purchase. So well satisfied were they with their theory, that they did not even discuss its application to any given year. They did not perceive that innumerable lags in the flow of money and in the flow of goods make that old theory of no practical use whatever. From their assumed premise they concluded, logically enough, that economics is concerned only with the problem of production: that consumption takes care of itself. Thus the orthodox economists, led by Adam Smith and John Stuart Mill, blinded by their own errors, intolerant of all opposing views, as hide-bound in their own field as their forefathers were in religion, forced upon the world a system of economics which, as far as it could, condemned mankind to intolerably slow progress; a system which is largely responsible for much, though by no means all, of the anxiety and suffering which our Little Gray Man has so much at heart — which we should *all* have painfully at heart, were it not for the fact that this very system of economics makes complacent hopelessness the mark of the educated man.'

The Business Man paused, and took his seat. All the other men, impressed with his depth of feeling and with the importance of the issue, were silent, expectant.

'Now,' he continued, 'having relieved my feelings with that blow, I expect the Professor to hit back.'

The Professor was ready. 'First of all,' he said, emphatically, 'most economists of to-day, though still loyal to Adam Smith and John Stuart Mill, do not believe that

they were right on all points. Far from it. Most economists are aware that the Automatic Theory, as embodied
in the *Wealth of Nations* and in Mill's *Principles*, does
not apply, without qualification, to any one month, or
even any one year. All *I* insist on — all most modern
economists insist on — is that the Automatic Theory is
sound in the long run.'

'And all *I* insist on ' — the counter-blow was swift and
straight — 'is that the Automatic Theory, when properly
qualified, means simply that whatever we do contrive to
produce — however meager, however far below poten-
tial capacity to produce — does somehow, sometime, get
used up. Such a theory, I hold, is no justification of
things as they are, and of no practical use whatever.'

The Business Man continued the attack: 'Supply and
demand would balance, even in short periods, in a world
of barter trading — a world in which goods are exchanged
solely against goods. In such a world, general overproduction — at least what I have meant by that term all
day — actually would be impossible, for the very reason
that general overproduction is purely a monetary matter. Consequently, as long as one ignores the medium of
exchange ——'

'The higher complications of the subject, as Jevons
rightly said,' interposed the Professor.

'Higher complications — nonsense!' the Business Man
replied. 'Money is not the surface of things. It is the
heart of the whole works. Anyway, as long as one ignores
money and thinks only of goods — chairs, matches,
Pullman towels, and the rest — he sees no possibility of
general overproduction; for the old economists were

right. In barter trading the balance between supply and demand always must be perfect, because the measure of demand *is* the supply.'

'Then you admit,' countered the Professor, quick to score on this opening, 'that the classical economists were right on that point.'

'Yes, on that point. But who ever lived in a barter economy? Nobody, as far as I can find out. Concentrate your study on a barter economy, as the classical economists did, and you miss the clue to the whole problem; for, until money is introduced, there is no problem; demand and supply really are one and the same thing, looked at from different viewpoints.'

'I get you,' nodded the Congressman. 'When a farmer brings a case of eggs to the cross-roads store, he adds a case of eggs to supply and also to demand. He may swap the eggs for calico cloth, but supply and demand are still equal.'

'That's the point.' The Business Man was evidently pleased with that way of putting it. 'Note, however, that it does not matter, for the purposes of my argument, whether or not you believe that general overproduction is impossible in a barter economy. All I ask you to believe is that the moment demand is expressed in money, the demand side of the market can be greatly increased or decreased any day, and often is, without reference to changes in the goods side of the market. So in a money economy there may be demand without supply or supply without demand; a seller's market or a buyer's market.'

'That may be for brief periods,' conceded the Professor, 'at least, with a certain use of your terms. I must say, however, that you use the terms "supply" and "demand" so vaguely that I am never sure exactly what you mean. Some one said the other day, "Teach a parrot to say 'supply and demand' and you have made a business man."'

'Some crack, that,' cried the Referee-Salesman. 'Do you claim a foul?'

'No, indeed. That was a fair hit. There is, of course, no such thing as demand or supply, except at a price. By "demand" I mean what every business man, parrot or no parrot, means by that term. I mean effective demand — dollars offered by buyers — and that is how I have meant to use the term all day. By *adequate* demand I mean enough consumer buying, sustained at high enough prices, to prevent a slump in the general level of retail prices. By "supply" I mean whatever is offered in exchange for the dollars, the total of consumers' commodities and services.'

The Lawyer looked perplexed. 'Still,' he said, 'that old theory about the inevitable balance of supply and demand always sounded reasonable to me. After all, modern trade *is* nothing but refined barter; money is merely a medium of exchange. In the last analysis, goods really are exchanged against goods; and no matter how large the volume becomes, somebody owns all the goods; so somebody has the means of payment.'

'Payment with goods, yes,' said the Business Man; 'but as a rule sellers do not want payment in goods. Anyway, most of the holders of goods are corporations, and corporations cannot do business by swapping goods. They have to have money.'

'Same with farmers; they can't get far swapping eggs for calico cloth.' The Congressman was still insisting that forty per cent of the population should not be left out. 'The fact that all the crops belong to some one does not mean that some one receives enough *money* income to buy them. I'm not much good at theory, but I do follow Government charts and reports, and I see right off the bat that there must be something wrong with that Automatic Theory, when the price-level goes up and down like a roller-coaster. Doesn't that in itself show that money does not go to consumers at the same rate as goods go to markets? Certainly people spend too little money at times and too much at other times.'

'Never spend too much for silk hosiery,' commented the Salesman.

'They spent a lot back in 1919,' said the Business Man.

'They sure did. Them was the good old days.'

'And so the stocking industry has been prosperous ever since?'

'Now you're kiddin' me. How could we make profits when the silk people stuck up the price of raw silk; everybody stuck up the price of everything else; and then prices went down with a bang, and we couldn't even get back the money we put into the hosiery? Rotten business ever since.'

'That's it,' the Business Man replied. 'But you don't seem to see that what you call "the good old days" had a lot to do with causing the rotten business, all because production does *not* automatically finance consumption.

Now, Professor, I want to make clear to you that I am not talking about temporary maladjustments which automatically correct themselves shortly, with little loss to society. I am talking about a long-run obstacle to progress. In order to see what I mean, imagine, if you will, a long chain of mammoth department stores, full of every conceivable thing for sale, and owned by millions of stockholders. How does the fact that they own the stores enable them to buy the goods?'

'Of course,' answered the Professor, 'they must first obtain enough money, as wages, or dividends, or in some other way.'

'But, as I have just explained, the production of a given volume of goods, in a given short period of time, does not provide consumers with enough money to buy those goods.'

'Why not?' asked the Lawyer. 'Our Salesman is not the only one beyond his depth now.'

So the Business Man restated the point in this way: 'No producer ever pays out in making goods as much money as he expects to receive for the goods, as much money as he *must* receive if he is to keep on producing goods. Isn't that clear? Did any one of you ever hear of a man who carried on business with the idea of making anything at a cost of a dollar and selling it for a dollar?'

'Never did visit a lunatic asylum,' said the Salesman. 'Have seen plenty of bankrupts, though, who did business that way. But they never intended to. How about it, Professor?'

The Professor admitted that producers of goods, as

long as they prosper, take in more money than they pay out as costs. He admitted, further, that there is a large part of their profits which they do not distribute as dividends.

'So I understand, Professor,' — for emphasis, the Business Man repeated his conclusion — 'I understand that you agree with me that the financing of the production of a given volume of goods in a given one- or two-year period does *not* automatically finance the consumption of those goods. Consequently, the people cannot buy all those goods unless they receive more money than is paid out in the production of the goods. In other words, the producers cannot sell all they make for more money than they pay out — cannot therefore go ahead producing — unless consumers get the necessary additional money from some other source. The shortage must be offset in some way.'

'But I cannot see,' objected the Professor, 'how the savings, either of corporations or of individuals, cause the shortage of which you speak. The money which industry receives from consumers and retains as undistributed profits is not locked up in strong boxes. Most of it is deposited in banks, where other men may borrow it and pay it out. So it flows on to consumers. That is true, also, of most of the money savings of individuals. Banks do not hoard money. They lend it as fast as they can. That is the only way they can do business.'

'Looks like a blow on the solar plexus,' exclaimed the Salesman.

'That won't faze him,' said the Gray Man.

'The dollars saved by certain individuals,' continued

the Professor, 'are invested by them and thus flow on to others in the process of creating new facilities or public works. Once you take account of the fact that money invested is money spent, you see that both individuals and corporations can save all they please without causing consumer buying to lag behind the production of consumers' goods.'

'Yes,' the Business Man replied, 'I am familiar with that contention, but it seems to me unsound. Of course it is true that a considerable part of money savings are deposited in banks, where the money is available for borrowers. But the fact that somebody *may* borrow the money and pay it out as wages, is immaterial as long as nobody *does* borrow it. Such money is no more a stimulus to business than is gold in the bowels of the earth.'

'As a matter of fact,' corroborated the Lawyer, from his experience as a bank director, 'a glance at bank statistics shows that bank loans fall off precisely when business is in greatest need of borrowers who will put the savings of depositors back into circulation.'

'That is my first answer to the Professor,' said the Business Man. 'My second answer is that even when money savings — whether or not first deposited in banks — are put back into circulation in the process of producing additional goods, the result may be still more trouble; for, as the Professor has just admitted, the process of producing such goods does not yield consumers enough money to buy even those goods, to say nothing of the goods which remained unsold in the first place, because the money in question was being saved instead of spent. Doesn't this double answer cover your point, Professor?'

The Professor rubbed his fingers thoughtfully over his chin. 'I think' — he said slowly, 'I think — yes, there is a real Dilemma of Thrift. Under certain conditions savings certainly do retard progress. But I still hold ——'

'Then you do admit' — the Business Man continued to follow up his case, point by point — 'then you do admit that all the money, including distributed profits, which is turned over to consumers in connection with putting a given volume of goods on the market, in any given year, is not enough to bring about the sale of those goods at prices which will induce continued production. You also admit, of course, that the deficit of consumer income must be made up in some way.'

'Yes, that follows.'

'Now, then, you recall my contention that the deficit is made up, if at all, by the expansion of money in connection with capital facilities and public works. Can you take that step with me?'

'Yes, I follow you there, but I don't ——'

'Just a minute, Professor. There will be plenty of time for your objections. First I want to find out just how far you can go with me. You agree that we cannot prosper unless consumers get the right amount of additional income through the building of capital facilities and public works.'

'I agree.'

'Now, then, do you contend that there is anything automatic about such developments which makes them yield approximately the additional income which consumers need?'

'No. Plainly there is not.'

'On the contrary, there are times when such developments yield consumers too much money; at other times, too little. No matter which way the movement is headed, once well started it is certain to go farther. Isn't that what happens?'

'Undoubtedly it is, but ——'

'Why all these "buts," Professor?' asked the Congressman. 'As far as I can see, you have now admitted the whole case, part by part.'

'Not the whole case, by any means.'

'Merely the top, bottom, and all the sides,' commented the Semi-Silk Salesman.

SECTION XII

'You are expecting too much of the Professor,' said the
Business Man. 'He has lived with his Theory all his
life. He doesn't want to throw it out of house and
home, all at once. And I don't want him to. First, I want
to ask him why economists fell into this basic error in the
first place, and why so many have stuck there ever since.
Is it not precisely because, having assumed that all trade
is essentially nothing but barter, they failed to understand the rôle of money? At least, you will admit, Professor, that John Stuart Mill made that failure; and that
he and his numerous disciples profoundly influenced
economic thought and teaching the world over.'

The Professor carefully filled his pipe and lighted it,
before he spoke. 'Yes, I suppose so,' he said, doubtfully. 'Now I come to think of it, Mill even went so far
as to say there cannot be "intrinsically a more insignifi-
cant thing in the economy of society than money, except
in the character of a contrivance for sparing time and
labor."'

'And that single sentence, although wrenched from its
context, fairly represents Mill's system of economics,'
said the Business Man. 'Guided by that thought, Mill
wrote the entire first volume of his *Principles of Economics* under the assumption that money did not exist;
and when he did introduce money, he failed to see just

how that complicated the problem of getting products into consumers' hands at the rate at which such products could be produced.'

'It is true,' the Professor readily admitted, 'that Mill neglected the very matters which you have been urging upon us to-day.'

'Which neglect,' the Business Man observed, 'is consistent with the assumption that production automatically finances sales. Once grant that, and you have to grant that business need not be concerned over the problem of getting goods consumed. There is no such problem. Look after production, and consumption will look after itself. Was not that precisely the view taken by the classical economists?'

'Yes, for the most part,' answered the Professor. 'Mill, himself, insisted that the limit of wealth is never deficiency of consumers, but of productive power. A general excess of all commodities above demand, he said, is an impossibility.'

'Leave things alone,' said the Congressman, 'and money will move around the circuit as the earth moves around the sun, without the aid of legislation. False on the face of it, I say, Professor. Looks to me as though this part of economic theory needed a new core.'

'If you can't stop this man soon, Professor, ain't goin' to be no core,' warned the Semi-Silk Salesman.

The Professor then remarked that, in fairness to economists of the present day, it should be said that most of them do not accept the traditional Automatic Theory as applied to short-term movements.

The Business Man said that he was well aware of that fact; but he pointed out that most of the writers who do not explicitly make that false assumption, nevertheless base their own theories upon it. 'Where,' he asked, 'do they show the extent to which the rejection of that assumption affects their views on innumerable practical matters — on the tariff, public works, payment of public debts, foreign loans, taxes, installment selling, to mention only a few? Isn't it a fact that various monthly bank letters, written by economists for the guidance of business men put forth that same old Theory, in one form or another, month after month?'

'I dare say,' he suggested, 'the Gentleman from Kansas has heard it even in Congress.'

'Even in Congress!'

'I cannot tell you how amazed I have been,' continued the Business Man, 'to find so many writers rejecting that old Theory, casually, and then going ahead as though nothing important had happened.'

'Just as if,' suggested the Congressman, 'a medieval sea-captain had thrown overboard the notion that the earth is flat, but failed to see how that need affect navigation.'

'Or as if,' added the Business Man, 'a mason couldn't tell a corner-stone when he saw one. Even those builders of economic systems who question the soundness of the Automatic Theory deal with the idea as though it were a surface ornament which could be removed and scrapped, like the frills of the Late General Grant Period of architecture, leaving the main structure still standing firmly. They do not see that the Automatic Theory is the corner-stone, not an ornament, and that they cannot remove it without toppling over the whole structure.'

'You are mistaken,' the Professor declared, 'if you suppose that Mill himself made that error. He says that his contention that general overproduction is impossible is fundamental. Difference of opinion on that point, he insists, involves radically different conceptions of political economy, especially in its practical aspect. Mill saw clearly that he could not reject that principle without rejecting very much more. On *his* view, he says, we have only to consider how to combine sufficient production with the best possible distribution; but on the *opposing* view, he says, there is a third thing to be considered — how a market can be created for produce. I have given you very nearly his own words.'

'And Mill, with his keenly logical mind, was right,' asserted the Business Man. 'Those who differ with him on that point have to build a new economics for guidance in practical affairs. If you doubt it, read almost any modern textbook. As you read, consider how much of the book, in the light of our discussion, has to be rewritten, and what a considerable part of the rest seems to be of no practical importance. More or less completely, economists have discarded the unifying principle which Mill insisted was fundamental. But I cannot see that they have agreed on any unifying principle to take its place. Refinements of statistical method and masses of statistics do not serve the purpose.'

'I see now,' said the Lawyer, 'what H. G. Wells probably had in mind, when he said that the old Political Economy made generalizations which were mostly

wrong, whereas the new Economics evades generalizations, and seems to lack the intellectual power to make
them.'

'That largely explains,' the Business Man remarked,
'why modern economics seems to most people so chaotic.
My own conviction is that a system of economics, cov-
ering its most practical aspects, might well be built
around the flow of money to consumers as the unifying
principle.'

The Congressman then turned to the Professor. 'Well,
Professor, what do you say about this theory now?'

'Exaggerated. Needs qualification at many points.
Nevertheless, I am frank to admit that there is much
more basis for the theory than I first thought.'

'And what do *you* say, Mr. Referee?'

'Pretty close to a technical knock-out. When any professor says that much, he's nearly taken the full count.'

But the Professor insisted that he was able to go several
more rounds.

'Then I should like to ask,' said the Lawyer, 'whether
there were not some men in the past century who de-
tected that error of orthodox economics.'

'Every age has its heretics,' answered the Business
Man. 'In the past century, various men saw that central
error; saw some merit even in the views of the lowly
mercantilists, ridiculed though these views were by the
lords of economic theory. But the heretics could not get
a hearing. The false theory held sway partly because it
was so respectably intrenched, partly because most of the
heretics did not see exactly why the flow of goods does
not rightly regulate the flow of money.'

'Did they not propose remedies?' asked the Lawyer.

'No practical remedies. Instead, they advocated the abolition of interest charges; or they sought to solve the problem by substituting "commodity money" for the gold standard; or they insisted that money could be stabilized and markets sustained merely by controlling the *gross* volume of money in circulation. Other reformers, precursors of the Soviet régime in Russia, sought to abolish private profits, individual initiative, and consumers' freedom of choice — a remedy which might, indeed, remove the chief causes of general overproduction, but only by removing, as well, one of the chief causes of progress. Still other reformers insisted that high wages and low prices would solve the problem.'

'How did these reformers explain the gains that were actually made?' the Lawyer asked, by way of further cross-questioning.

'They did not account for them at all. In fact, their arguments proved too much: proved that substantial gains were impossible. Moreover, none of these reformers offer any explanation of how the deficiency of income arises, or any way of supplying the deficiency, which is convincing to the leaders in business and politics. These leaders are themselves hampered in their efforts to find a way out because, in their school days, they studied scarcely any economics except that of Adam Smith and John Stuart Mill and their disciples; and, ever since, they have been too busy to think out a system of economics which squares with their own experience. So the difficulty of getting goods consumed has never thrust itself upon them as a major problem of economics, separate and distinct from the problem of getting goods produced.'

Whereupon, in answer to an invitation to proceed with the cross-examination, the Lawyer declared that he was through.

'But I am not,' insisted the Professor. 'I hold that you have not yet told the whole story.'

'Too long a story, I fear, even at that,' said the Business Man.

'One of us is no longer bored.' The Congressman grinned, and pointed to the Semi-Silk Salesman, slumped in the corner, sound asleep, and looking rounder than ever. 'He knows how to knit up the raveled sleeve of care — stockings, I should say.'

The Little Gray Man, who had listened to the lengthy discussion intently, hopefully, and silently, now declared that his own question had been fully answered. 'It is plain,' he said, 'why nothing far-reaching has ever been done toward controlling the flow of money. Of course, anybody who accepts the orthodox theory thereby rejects all theories which are consistent with the Plain Facts. He can no more see the truth than men who are convinced that the earth is flat can see the evidence rolling through the heavens that the earth is round.'

'In other words,' said the Congressman, 'if a man accepts the Earth-is-Flat Theory of Consumption — if he is convinced that supply itself creates adequate demand — he naturally devotes his full attention to supply.'

'And so becomes production-mad,' added the Gray Man.

'Yes; and so for him, as well as for the other followers of Adam Smith and John Stuart Mill,' the Business Man concluded, 'there is no such thing as a problem of financing consumption. Production itself does the trick. For the same reason, there is no such thing as a Dilemma of Thrift. Go ahead preaching unlimited savings, for it is impossible for any country to save too much. It does not matter how much is saved, because all savings are used in producing something, and thereby, as the Professor tried to convince us, provide consumers with enough money to buy it. If you believe all that, you naturally conclude that the only financial system any country needs is a system of financing production.'

'If you tie up to that old bunk,' said the Congressman, 'you see no reason why the Government should not go ahead borrowing money, spending money, planning public works, levying taxes, regulating tariffs, without any regard to the way these measures affect the money income of consumers.'

'Yes,' added the Business Man, 'and adjourning, as Congress did last year, without passing appropriation bills for pensions and public works; as though the Government could hold back as many millions as it pleased without affecting business. Why try to take care of anything which takes care of itself? Why interfere with the operation of a beneficent economic law?

'You see,' he went on, 'it is all consistent. Let a man grant the false premise and he has to accept the rest. That makes him ——'

'It makes him a philosopher,' interrupted the Congressman; 'a blind man, in a dark cellar, hunting for a black cat that isn't there.'

'Or, rather, a man of normal vision, in the full light of day, hunting for a pussy cat at his feet — but hunting in vain because of the thick, black bandage which is tied over his eyes.'

'And that bandage' — the light in the Congressman's eyes showed that something amused him — 'that bandage is the Earth-is-Flat Theory of Consumption. A kind of parlor game. Put the bandage over the victim's eyes, and he stumbles around, holding the donkey's tail in front of him, and coming a dozen times within easy reach of the right place to pin it; but he is just as likely eventually to pin the tail on the donkey's ear or on the parlor lamp, as anywhere else.'

'Adam Smith illustrates that perfectly,' said the Business Man. 'Having covered his eyes with a dark fallacy, he proceeds to grope around the economic world, again and again walking right up to the place he is seeking, holding out his hand so close to it that there seems no possibility of his missing it; then off he goes in the wrong direction. He even concludes that the United States cannot prosper by expanding manufactures, but only by expanding agriculture. Blinded in the same way, Mill takes the wrong course again and again. Instead of seeing that international trade is a cause of war, he insists that it must be a cause of peace. He concludes that "low wages do not cause low prices, nor high wages, high prices." He even goes so far wrong as to say that a rise of wages in general must decrease profits, for there is no alternative. For the same reason, he can see no difference between new

money paid as wages by manufacturers and new money
put into circulation by governments; although, as I have
explained, one tends to create a deficit of consumer demand and the other an excess. As a result ——'

The Professor again interrupted to remark that this account was not the whole story.

'Still, if I remember correctly,' said the Lawyer, 'Mill
concludes that wages in any country are habitually at the
lowest rate to which the laborer will suffer them to be de-
pressed, rather than put a restraint upon birth-rate.'

'And having thus shown that wages in general must
always tend toward the lowest level of subsistence,' the
Business Man remarked, 'Mill rounds out a complete
Economics of Despair.'

'Wrong,' asserted the Professor positively. 'Mill be-
lieved firmly in economic progress; he was a professed
optimist.'

'Yes; if you can call a man an optimist whose theories
are enough to drive millions of wage-earners to despair.
Mill, in effect, shuts off the view where there is most
hope, and then commends complacent acceptance of
misery.'

'In which respect,' commented the Gray Man, 'he is
much like the learned Bishop.'

'I have his name at last, Bernstein — Jake Bernstein!'
exclaimed the Salesman, jounced awake by a sudden
lurch of the car.

'That *would* shock the Bishop,' chortled the Congressman, 'even if the misery of the poor doesn't.'

The Semi-Silk Salesman yawned and stretched his
arms. 'Economics too deep for me; better try pinochle;

guess Jake was right,' he said, as he started for the door. 'Anyway,' he added, pulling the green curtain aside, 'knock his eye out when I tell him about the Monocrypto-cidal Theory of Kitchenettes.'

The Business Man laughed. 'I dare say we'd all admit we were tired,' he said, 'if we were all frank. Anyway, if you will excuse me, I'll see if there is anything I can do for my wife.'

'But ——,' began the Gray Man.

'No, I'm not deserting you. I'll come back soon and join the survivors, if there are any.'

Even the Gray Man was glad to have a change. Again he stood alone on the platform, looking through the door. Again he saw row upon row of shabby houses that told the story of long and futile struggles to rise above anxiety and want. Again, through the factory windows, he saw row upon row of toilers.

Luckily for them, he thought, much of the gloom has been dispelled from what men rightly called the Dismal Science. By what blasting of hopes it earned that name! By 'proving' that 'natural laws' prevent the human race from rising far above want. By taking over from the darkest age of theology the doctrine of original sin, and ascribing poverty to the natural depravity of the workers. By insisting that out of the skies comes the curse of un-employment. By warning men that it is useless to try to escape from trammels of their own creation. In short, by darkening counsel in much that pertains to well-being.

Hopeless it certainly is — at least the economics which most of us were taught in college. The greatest prosperity it conceives to be possible is never prosperity for the under dog. It gives to many of those who have a plenty what seems to them a sufficient excuse for shutting their eyes to the plight of the poor. And so even the Kindly Lawyer was led to say, 'What, after all, can be done about it? Not much of anything.'

SECTION XIII

IN WHICH IT BECOMES CLEAR THAT CONGRESS ITSELF HAS SHOWN THE NEED OF A GUIDING POLICY

THE Little Gray Man was back in the smoking-room, talking with the Congressman and the Lawyer, when the Business Man returned.

'Here you are,' said the Gray Man, 'just in time to help us out. We still can't understand why so many people have accepted this old economics.'

'Easy to understand as far as business men are concerned: they haven't accepted it all, in practice. As theorists, to be sure, they hold that production, as long as it is balanced production, furnishes plenty of buyers; so nobody need be concerned about markets. They are, nevertheless, greatly concerned about markets. They laud Adam Smith, who contended that the United States cannot prosper by developing manufactures; whereupon they devote their energies chiefly to expanding manufactures. Urge business men to stand firmly by the long-established system of economics, and they will respond warmly. Tell them that our prosperity depends on protection, and they will respond even more warmly. Yet——'

'Yet the two positions are contradictory!' the Congressman exclaimed.

'That's just it,' continued the Business Man. 'Many men adopt in theory a system of economics which in practice they largely reject. As students, they accept doctrines which logically require the acceptance of free trade; but as men of affairs, they are out-and-out protectionists. Then, too, they have no concern as theorists over a favorable balance of trade; but as business men, they insist on it with almost religious zeal.'

The Congressman remarked that he knew from experience how to explain that conflict. 'Business men,' he said, 'usually take the judgment of experts in matters in which they are not experts; and they haven't taken time to make themselves experts in economic theory.'

'There may be another reason for this conflict between what they say and what they do,' the Lawyer suggested. 'Business men have found certain parts of orthodox economics useful as bulwarks to hold back floods of discontent; while at the same time, they have found it easy to ignore the parts which are inconsistent with what they want to do.'

'Fortunately so,' said the Business Man. 'Suppose they had been governed in practice by the theory that nothing need be done toward creating markets except providing the markets with goods. Suppose they had accepted the conclusion that it is impossible to raise wages without reducing profits; impossible to lift the masses of workers far above the bare level of subsistence!'

'Luckily, they haven't,' the Congressman remarked. 'Instead, they've gone ahead doing the impossible. What the pioneers in the automobile industry have done for us, other business men in other industries have done for previous generations.'

'Especially,' added the Business Man, 'during the

hundred and fifty years since certain fallacies were so
effectively expounded in the *Wealth of Nations.*'

'How about it?' The Congressman turned to the Professor, who had just come back to the smoking-room.
'Don't you think business men deserve something more
than scorn from professors?'

'No doubt, but there are still some important objections ——'

'All of which we want to hear,' said the Business Man.
'But first I wish you would let me sum up what I have
been trying to say about the Proposed Plan.'

The Business Man then summarized the discussion.
Progress, he said, can come only when there is the right
flow of money to consumers. The flow is not right unless
in some way the shortage due to corporate and individual savings is made up, and unless there is, in addition,
a sufficient flow of *new* money to bring about the distribution of a constantly increasing output. In the past, the
right flow of money actually has come at times, but never
for many months running. The reason why nothing has
been done, in a large way, to substitute control for chance,
is because it has always been assumed that nothing need
be done — that production itself induces the right flow of
money to consumers; that there is therefore no such
thing as a Dilemma of Thrift; in short, no such thing as
the problem under discussion.

That false assumption is at the very core of the traditional economics of distribution. It prevented men from
looking in the right direction for a solution of the problem. More than that, up to the present time it has pre-

vented most men, economists and business men alike,
from even admitting that there is any such problem.
But now that we see the falsity of the traditional assumption — see, therefore, the nature of the problem — there
is no reason why we should not find a simple solution.

'What we must have,' the Business Man declared, 'is a
solution of the problem which is radical, in that it goes to
the bottom of the difficulty; a solution which is revolutionary, in that it involves the overthrow of accepted
ideas and the adoption of an entirely new controlling purpose. But we must have a solution which is at the same
time conservative, in that it leaves unchanged all those
established institutions which are generally regarded as
essential; a solution which is commonplace, in that it requires us to do little more than we are already doing.'

'Some paradox!' exclaimed the Congressman. 'A way
out which is radical and revolutionary, while being conservative and commonplace!'

'Impossible as that may sound,' said the Business
Man, 'I hope to convince you all that there is such a
way out.'

The Business Man then went on to explain what he
meant by saying that his Proposed Policy is both conservative and radical. It is conservative, he said, because
it involves no changes in the essentials of the established
order. It leaves individual initiative, responsibility, and
rewards, throughout the whole domain of commerce and
finance, exactly where they are to-day. It does not provide for the taking over by the Government of any functions now adequately performed by private agencies.

The Proposed Policy could be put into operation at

once, without any changes in banking and currency laws, or in the gold reserve ratio, or in any other phase of the Federal Reserve System. It could be put into effect whether or not any changes are made in tariffs or taxes, and whether or not there is any special farm legislation. The new Policy does propose to do away with the extremes of business depression and unemployment, but few regard these as necessary for the success of the established order.

All that the project asks us to do is to start with what we now have, and go a little farther, cautiously, watchfully, all the while measuring results. Thus we can find out from experience how much or how little is necessary to achieve the desired ends. In this respect, the Policy is evolutionary, in full accord with Anglo-Saxon ways of progress.

The Business Man then emphasized the fact that what he advocated was thus seen to be in marked contrast with most proposals for far-reaching improvements. Such proposals usually involve upheavals of the established order; Government control of all industry, for example, or the abolition of private banking, or of private ownership of land, or of private profits. The proponents of such disruptive methods, like the searchers in Poe's story of *The Purloined Letter*, seem to think that it is necessary to rip up the whole house, when all the while the letter they are looking for is lying in plain sight. All sorts of revolutionists may well be opposed to the new Policy, because it takes away some of their chief arguments.

'In short,' concluded the Business Man, 'the Proposed Policy is moderate and simple.'

'Too simple, I fear,' said the Professor.

'Isn't that one of its chief merits?'

'Decidedly so,' answered the Congressman. 'At first I thought you were going to advocate commodity money, or fiat money, or some other one of the wild schemes which some crazy galoot is always writing me about. I am relieved, rather than disappointed, to find that your Policy *is* simple.'

'That's the way I feel about it,' said the Gray Man. 'When I couldn't start my Ford, the day I wanted to take some kiddies to the circus, and looked all over the blamed thing for a loose screw, and lay on my back in the dirt hunting for a hidden cause of the trouble, and felt like trying a sledgehammer on it, and then discovered that all the car needed was gasoline, I didn't complain that the solution was too simple.'

That reminded the Congressman of what the scoffers said when Columbus returned from his first voyage to the New World: "Nothing wonderful about that; all he did was to sail west until he reached land, and then sail east until he reached home." Christopher was right there with an answer — at least, according to the story. He asked if any one of those present knew how to stand an egg on its end. After all, including the Queen, had tried and failed, he took an egg, rapped it gently on the end, breaking the shell, and then stood it up. "Simple enough," he said, "when you know how."'

'A good analogy for your purpose,' said the Business Man. 'But note where the analogy falls down. Columbus started out on unknown seas to do what no man had ever done before; whereas I propose that we stay in familiar paths and do little more than we are now doing. Doing it all, however,' he added, placing much emphasis on this point, 'with a definite object in view. That is where the adventure comes in. That is where the hope lies of discovering a new economic world.'

'As I understand it,' said the Congressman, 'you propose that, in both public and private business, we should take due account of the fact that certain acts — paying off Government debts, for example, building public works, and speeding up the construction of new industrial plants — are good for business at certain times, and bad for business at other times.'

'Which means, as I understand it,' commented the Gray Man, 'that we should know when to put the foot on the brake and when to put it on the accelerator.'

'But society is not a machine,' objected the Professor. 'You cannot control human beings by pushing a lever.'

'Nevertheless,' the Business Man rejoined, 'I hope to show you that the Gray Man is right. Take an example from current financing. The Federal Government recently called long-term bonds to the value of billions of dollars and sold short-term certificates of indebtedness. That is said to have been the largest single financial transaction in history. I do not need to trace all the influences of that transaction on the volume and flow of money, in order to convince you that the effects on consumer income must have been far-reaching. Yet such possible effects, as far as I can learn, were not taken into consideration.'

'Probably not,' said the Congressman.

'Now the point is,' the Business Man continued, 'that the Government had the option of doing that huge piece of financing then or later on; or it might have done a part at that time, and then measured the results, in order to find out whether it was the right time to complete the transaction. That is only one of a hundred cases I might use to illustrate the practical working of the Proposed Policy.'

'Another case in point,' said the Congressman, 'is the Bonus Bill. It seems to me now, in the light of our discussion, that the one thing above all others which Congress should have considered was the probable effect of the proposed bonus payments on the volume of consumer buying, and the consequent effect on general well-being. Was it the time to apply the brakes or to step on the gas? Such a bill, going into effect at one time, would benefit the whole country, including the ex-service men; at another time, it would injure the whole country, including the ex-service men. What would have been the effect on general business conditions at the time in question? That was the main issue. Yet it was submerged under petty issues during those weary months when the bill was hanging fire.'

'You have summed it all up for us.' The Business Man evidently liked that way of explaining it. 'The gist of our Policy is to know when to put the foot on the brake and when to put it on the accelerator.'

'On that issue, you must be right,' said the Lawyer. 'However, if I may now change the subject, I should like to remind you that most business men contend that there is already too much interference with private business on the part of the Government.'

'And I agree with them,' quickly rejoined the Business Man. 'What I propose is less official interference with business. I don't know how to emphasize that fact sufficiently — unless I have it painted in red on those billboards out there. Don't you see that the very best way for the Government to avoid interfering with business is to be guided in all its own financial operations by the principles we have been discussing — putting more money into consumers' hands when business is falling off, and less money when inflation is under way?'

'In any event,' commented the Congressman, 'as I said at the outset, our Government is the largest consumer in the world, and as such inevitably helps or hinders business. The question is not whether the Government shall influence business, but how intelligently. At least it should try to exert its influence on the right side.'

'So the Government should adopt long-range planning of public works for the purpose of stabilizing employment,' said the Professor. 'That part of your Proposed Policy, at least, I fully endorse. Certainly, it is sound policy in periods of rapid expansion of business to curtail or postpone Government construction, as far as practicable, and to increase Government expenditures for public works when employment is falling off. That, however, is nothing more than economists have long favored, not only in this country, but in various other countries.'

'And that is one theory, at least,' added the Lawyer, 'upon which business men agree with economists. Back

in 1923, the President's Conference on Unemployment
reported in favor of planning construction work long in
advance with reference to cyclical movements of business,
and passing the necessary appropriations for such work
whenever statistics show that business needs the help of
increased public expenditures. Many chambers of commerce and business men generally have endorsed that
policy.'

'Also the American Federation of Labor,' said the Gray
Man.

'And many Government officials, as well.' The Congressman reminded the men of what Secretary Mellon had
said about the gains that could be made for the taxpayers
if governments would not compete for labor and materials
at times when both are scarce, and about the stabilizing
effect on business if such works as have been planned
could be built largely when there is a slowing-down of
industry.

'President Coolidge and Secretary Hoover have expressed similar views; and if I remember rightly,' the
Lawyer remarked, 'there was a plank in the Democratic
National platform calling for legislation to authorize the
construction and repair of public works in periods of acute
unemployment.'

'Yes,' said the Business Man, 'and what are the practical results to date of this remarkable unanimity of opinion? Virtually no results at all.'

'It is easy to see why,' the Lawyer explained, 'for without the guidance of your analysis, nothing *could* be done.
There would be no means of knowing what to do, or when
to do it.'

'That's it,' said the Business Man. 'And of course you see the other reason why nothing has been done. Nobody is responsible for carrying out the policy and nobody has the power; whereas every business man knows that the only way to get anything done is to give somebody adequate power and hold him responsible for results. This is a case where everybody agrees that it would be fine if somebody else would do something, yet scarcely anybody does anything.'

'Exactly the situation,' commented the Congressman.

'As it is now,' the Business Man continued, 'each and every branch of the Government is properly concerned with its own affairs, for which it is alone responsible. It is only remotely concerned with the general problem of maintaining the right flow of money to consumers.'

'And each branch of the Government,' added the Congressman, 'is doing less within its own field than it wants to do, because — as I hear every day — a short-sighted Congress has failed to provide appropriations commensurate with each department's idea of the importance of its own work.'

'Like any other group of human beings,' commented the Professor, 'a department of a university, for example.'

'Or a division of a corporation.' The Business Man spoke from long experience. 'And so,' he concluded, 'it is stupid to expect that any agency of the Government will curtail its own activities, in the supposed interest of business in general.'

'If it did,' remarked the Congressman, 'take my word, its reward would be reduced appropriations. Practically, the situation is this: no department has any money to spend which has been appropriated with a view to stabilizing business; no department has sufficient leeway in the use of its funds to accomplish much, even if it wanted to do so; and in any event, no department knows enough to tell just when to act in the interest of business in general.'

'As long as such conditions prevail,' exclaimed the Gray Man, 'everybody might talk himself blue in the face about the advantages of allocating public expenditures with reference to the needs of business, without having the slightest effect on business.'

'The only reason why such conditions *do* prevail,' — the Business Man spoke with conviction on this point — 'is because Congress has no comprehension of the magnitude or importance of the matter. That is evident from the bill which was introduced last winter — by Senator Pepper, I believe.'

'Perhaps,' suggested the Congressman, 'you refer to the amendment which Senator Pepper offered to the appropriation bill of the Department of Agriculture. That bill carried seventy-one million dollars for roads; and the Senator proposed to have the amount doubled in any year in which the volume of general construction in the United States should fall one third below the volume of 1926, over a period of three successive months.'

'That proposal is a step in the right direction,' said the Business Man. 'It ought to lead to a thorough study of the whole problem. But such a study will show that, in considering nothing more than Senator Pepper's proposal, Congress is merely trifling with a very serious matter. That is evident from our discussion to-day. By the time construction in general had fallen off one third,

and stayed at that low level for three months, business
would be in the depths of depression. Then it would be
too late to help matters much by spending a paltry seventy-one million dollars, no matter how the money was
spent. Such an amount, if spent in the nick of time, might
be sufficient. But what could have been accomplished in
1921, for example, when wages fell off seven billion dollars, by spending an additional seventy-one million dollars on roads? You might thereby have repaired — well,
say one per cent of the damage already done — nothing
more. That is what I mean by saying that even if Senator
Pepper's plan had been adopted, Congress would have
been trifling with the problem.'

'But don't be too hard on Congress,' pleaded the Gentleman from Kansas. 'What can you expect Congress to
do? Without the guidance you propose, Congress can't
do anything at the right time, because it has no means of
knowing when the right time comes.'

'True. As a matter of fact, the Pepper Amendment is
significant for two main reasons: first, because it shows
that some members of Congress are beginning to study
both the flow of money in its bearing on prosperity and
the relation of Government expenditures to the flow of
money; and second, because the way in which that
amendment was discussed shows that as yet Congress
has no conception of the nature or the magnitude of the
problem.'

'This discussion of the Pepper Amendment,' said the
Lawyer, 'brings home to me, better than anything else
you have said, the need and probable effectiveness of just

such a guiding Policy as you propose. And now, if I may
be a witness in my own behalf, I will say frankly that I
was mistaken in the discouraging views I first expressed.
I certainly should not have spoken as I did this morning
if I had seen the whole matter as I now see it. Most of
my doubts have been cleared up. I see now, as I never
saw before, that both legislators and economists have
long failed to understand the rôle of money in the
world's work, and I am now fully convinced that your
theory is sound.'

'Hear! Hear!' cried the Congressman.

'Still, it seems to me that you, on your part, exaggerate
the importance of money. After all, our increased production is due to invention, discovery of new resources,
growth of capital savings, growth of bank funds available
for producers, also the result of savings, increase in the
average productive life of laborers, and ——'

'And there are many other factors,' interrupted the
Business Man, 'without which we could not have
reached the present volume of production. But which is
the *limiting factor?* That is the question to ask for practical guidance. If it takes equal parts of ten different ele-
ments to make a given compound, the quantity which
you can make will be determined by that one element of
which you have the smallest supply. It avails nothing
to increase the supply of the other nine. So it usually is
with the output of industry.'

'So it is at the present moment,' the Congressman said
earnestly. 'The limiting factor cannot be labor, for
several million workers are unemployed and several million more are employed only on part time. The limiting

factor cannot be capital equipment, for virtually every
industry complains that it is over-equipped. Neither can
the limiting factor be available producers' funds, since
our banks have been forced to accumulate bonds, for lack
of commercial borrowers. And, as you all well know, we
are far from making full use of our land, our raw materials,
our water power, or our inventions.'

'And surely,' added the Business Man, 'the limiting
factor is not knowledge of how to produce nor productive
power. The limiting factor must be consumer income.
Certainly the volume of production is limited by the volume of consumption, and certainly the volume of consumption is limited by consumer income.'

'If you don't mind using my old Ford car again for an
illustration,' said the Gray Man, 'consider the situation
the day when I couldn't make the car go. There was the
machine, in good order, waiting to be used. There were
the roads, all constructed. There were the kiddies, eager
to go to the circus. There was the chauffeur, somewhat
begrimed and overheated, to be sure, but ready to do
his part. It wouldn't be exaggerating to say that the one
thing needed was fuel. You don't have to go any further
to convince *me* that there are times when a large part of
our industrial machinery is in the same position. And
the only fuel it needs is more money spent by consumers.'

'It has just occurred to me' — the Congressman was
fumbling through his numerous papers again — 'that I
have an equally good illustration. Here is a picture I had
taken in New York the other day by the Photomaton.
Remarkable invention of a penniless Russian Jew immi-
grant — a millionaire now, I reckon. You walk into the

shop. There is the machine, all set up, with every necessary means of production except one. Machine idle. Try
to cram too much money in the slot — nothing doing; not
enough money — nothing doing. But drop a quarter in
the slot. Presto! All the agencies of production get to
work at once, and out comes your photograph. There you
have it: a working model of the industrial world. Isn't
that so, Professor?'

'Not so simple as that,' insisted the Professor. 'In the
real world, mental attitudes as well as money determine
when the wheels go round.'

But just then the wheels of a passing freight train went
round with such roar and rattle that the conversation had
to cease.

SECTION XIV

IN WHICH, AT LAST, THE PROFESSOR IS CONVINCED
THAT THERE IS A ROAD TO PLENTY

'Now that we can make ourselves heard —— ' the Business Man began, turning to the Professor.

'All I started to say,' the Professor answered, 'is that confidence in the business outlook does help to bring on a revival of business.'

'Yes, even a sunshine campaign may start business; but only consumers' dollars can sustain it.'

The Salesman returned just in time to hear that remark. 'Sure thing,' he agreed. 'Self-starter saves time startin' the engine. Takes a steady flow of gasoline to keep it goin'.'

'That's it,' said the Business Man. 'Industry cannot run on optimism. Optimism cannot create commodities or sell them; it cannot operate a shoe factory or take shoes off the retailers' shelves. It must first induce somebody to spend money.'

'So,' the Congressman concluded, 'the sunshine cure for business anæmia is a quack remedy.'

'The only real remedy,' repeated the Business Man, 'is the right flow of money to consumers. Take care of that and public confidence will take care of itself. If, on the other hand, you induce men to prepare for a volume of consumer demand that is not forthcoming, you only make matters worse.'

'That may be,' said the Professor, 'but does not con-

fidence in the business outlook lead men to borrow more
money, employ more workers, build new factories, order
more machinery, and thus achieve your very purpose by
the very means you advocate?'

The Congressman chuckled. 'Take my word,' he said,
'the Professor has you on that point. Your *own* Plan is
designed to keep men confident.'

'Yes,' replied the Business Man, 'confident that demand will grow fast enough; but also confident that it
will not grow too fast. As things now go, the time is sure
to come when demand outruns supply and prices begin
to rise. Then, without more restraints than we have had
in the past, speculation will run riot, stocks will be held
back for still higher prices, rising costs will encroach on
profits, and sooner or later a collapse will come ; all due
to continued excess of consumer income, which could
have been prevented by the Policy which we are considering.'

'In any event,' the Professor admitted, 'it would be
folly to try to sustain business by endeavoring directly to
measure and control anything as intangible as states of
mind; whereas the Plan you propose deals only with
tangible things, easily measured.'

'Well, then,' cried the Gray Man, with growing impatience, 'aren't you ready to join us in trying to get somewhere?'

'Yes, Professor, doesn't that clear up all your doubts?'
asked the Congressman.

'Not all. I still cannot see how the right flow of money
in general would help those particular industries which
most need help. Suppose consumers received larger in-

comes next month. They would spend very little more for textiles, leather, and farm products.'

'That point has been covered already,' declared the Lawyer. 'The Plan we are discussing aims to prevent *general* overproduction. No plan whatever can prevent the overproduction of individual commodities — at least, as long as consumers are free to choose and producers are free to take chances. Even when business in general is highly prosperous, some industries are sure to be in distress; but that does not prevent general economic progress.'

'In any event,' said the Business Man, 'each producer and each industry must be left to guard, as best they can, against relative overproduction. At present they have that problem to solve and in addition all the problems that go with general business depressions and the fear of them.'

'The least we must say,' the Congressman insisted, 'is that even those industries which are *relatively* overproduced are better off in good times than in hard times. You don't need to remind any one from Kansas that the farmers are in relatively hard luck right now; but at least they are better off than they would be in the depths of a general business depression. Come now, Professor, admit that you are convinced, and make the vote unanimous.'

'Well, I don't want to weary you with further objections,' said the Professor. 'Perhaps we ought to call off the discussion, and hear the story of the blind beggar. But I must say we haven't yet considered the matter from every angle.'

'For example?'

'The importance of having enough buyers for producers' goods. All you propose to do is to sustain the demand for consumers' goods. But is not the production of shoe machinery that cannot be sold as serious a matter as the production of shoes that cannot be sold? If manufacturers stop buying machinery and materials on account of lack of confidence in the future, may there not be a business depression, even though consumers continue to buy as usual?'

'I am glad you raised that point,' said the Business Man, 'for it is a common objection. The answer, however, is simple. Adequate consumer demand in itself sustains adequate producer demand. In other words, there cannot possibly be a surplus of producers' goods as long as consumers continue to buy the output of finished goods; but there can easily be a surplus of finished goods, even though producers' demand keeps up with the output of producers' goods.'

'Producers' goods in general?' asked the Lawyer.

'Yes. The problem of *general* overproduction is the only one I have discussed to-day. Even under the Policy I propose, there might be a surplus of any one type of producers' goods — textile machinery, for example, or hides, or pig-iron.'

'Or raw silk,' added the Salesman. 'Not sure that I get your point, though.'

'Then let me drive it home by stating a fact that is perfectly well known to every one of you: Consumers never stop buying because they fear a slump in the market for producers' goods; but producers periodically stop buying because they fear a slump in the market for consumers' goods.'

'That certainly does drive the point home,' admitted the Professor. 'It largely meets my objection.'

'The underlying reason,' the Lawyer explained, 'is that all profits, all the way from oil well and ranch to filling-station and restaurant, are accumulated in retail prices. Consequently, nothing but adequate retail buying can keep industry going all the way down the line. That is why the using-up of consumers' goods sufficiently stimulates the demand for producers' goods. That is why the reverse is not true.'

'All of which,' concluded the Business Man, 'follows naturally from the fact that the using-up of consumers' goods is the end of economic activity, while the using-up of producers' goods is only one means toward that end.'

'Very well,' conceded the Professor, 'I grant that the right flow of money to consumers is all that is needed to keep business prosperous. But *your* way of keeping the flow right is not the only way. *Anything* that will reduce the cyclical oscillations of industry will keep consumer purchasing power better adjusted to current output. Anything that will *eliminate* the cyclical oscillations of industry will largely, though not wholly, keep consumer purchasing power and current output in proper adjustment.'

'Granted,' the Business Man replied. 'And I am proposing immediately practical and far-reaching measures for accomplishing that very purpose. What do *you* propose?'

'Well, for one thing,' the Professor suggested, 'I propose that banks require business borrowers to show an
improving current ratio in periods of activity.'

'In general that is a good idea,' agreed the Business
Man. 'But you are well aware that to carry out that idea
by drastic restrictions on the lending power of banks
would do more harm than good. On the other hand, you
couldn't get far merely by commending the idea to the
banks. There are practical difficulties in the way: fixed
commitments, obligations to depositors, danger of losing
customers to other banks — to mention only a few.'

'Nevertheless, the idea is sound,' insisted the Professor.

'I agree with you. I grant, too, that there are other
measures which would help. Some of them, no doubt,
ought to be tried. All I say is that economists have proposed nothing which is practical and at the same time so
far-reaching as the Plan which we are discussing. Am I
not right, Professor?'

'Perhaps so, in the main. Still — if I may now take up
a new point — there is no assurance that the people will
buy the right things, just because they are able to. Consider how they have spent their increased wages since
1914. What good will it do them to buy still more cos-
metics and cigarettes and automobiles and motion pictures?' The Professor punctuated his list of extravagances
with staccato taps of his pipe on the window sill. 'And
boot-leggers' liquor,' he added, with a still more expres-
sive tap. 'This book by Professor Carver, which I brought
to read on the train, shows a danger which prosperity has
brought to our wage-earners — the danger of self-indul-
gence and a breakdown of ——'

'Gr-e-a-t Jupiter!' exclaimed the Gray Man. 'I did not expect that of *you!* Sounds like the learned Bishop. What is your own experience, Professor? No doubt you have twice as much income as you used to have. Has that demoralized you and your family? You have two or three times as much income as the great majority of wage-earners. Would *you* be better off with less money, because you don't spend it for the right things?'

'That's a knock-out,' chuckled the Congressman.

'Even so,' the Business Man explained, 'it doesn't hit the argument in its weakest spot. We must grant that there is much foolish spending of money. But education is the only remedy for that. We are not offering our new Policy as a substitute for education. In the future, as in the past, it will take time for people to learn how to spend their increased wages to the best advantage. How can they ever learn as long as their energies must be used up in gaining a bare living?'

'And how,' asked the Gray Man, 'can any one ever learn to spend a little more money wisely, except by having a little more money to spend?'

'There is no other way,' the Business Man declared. 'Whenever people suddenly find themselves with more money to spend than they ever had before — in California gold-rush days, for example, and in the War years — some people are certain to spend money foolishly, and their folly is certain to attract attention. But note that the economic progress which makes such extravagant spending possible also makes universal education possible.'

'That means,' commented the Gray Man, 'that everything we can do in the future to guarantee the people,

not only a living wage, not only a saving wage, but also
a culture wage, will help them to find out how to spend
their money for the more durable satisfactions of life.'

'Education is the only hope,' agreed the Lawyer.
'You cannot do much by law to improve public tastes.
Nobody would tolerate having the Government decide
for him how he must spend his money. Consumers must
remain free to decide by their dollar votes, cast daily in
the markets, what the machinery of the country is to
turn out. The function of our economic organization is
not to determine what the people *ought* to want, but to
make the machinery as productive as possible of what
they *do* want. So it seems to me, Professor, that your
objection is beside the point.'

'By no means beside the point,' the Professor replied,
positively. 'We are discussing the Gray Man's problem
— in his own words, how to guarantee the workers more
of the durable satisfactions of life. More money is not the
only solution. You don't have to overlook the Bishop's
side of the case, just because he overlooked yours.'

'Granted; fully granted,' said the Business Man.

'Will you also grant that an increased flow of money
cannot achieve your purpose, if it flows to the wrong
people? Suppose the surfeited rich, who already have
larger incomes than they care to spend, get still more
money. How does that help merchants to clear their
over-stocked shelves? May not the very fact that the
rich save too much prevent the success of your Plan?'

'That's just the point I started out with,' the Business
Man said, eagerly. 'The only way society can make use
of the savings of the rich, is by seeing to it that the rest

of the people have enough money to spend. Until they *do*
have enough, as shown by current indexes, our Policy op-
erates to yield them more. When the flow is right, that
fact becomes evident. Then no one need worry about
excess savings, for every one can save as much as he
pleases, without causing a shortage of consumer buying.'

'Even then,' the Professor insisted, 'many of the
neediest would be unable to buy, for there are economic
causes of misery which cannot be reached by your Policy.'

That point, too, the Business Man fully conceded. He
spoke of the mental defectives, of the shiftless and the
irresponsible, whose chief troubles are beyond the reach
of financial mechanisms. There is also, he said, an ir-
reducible minimum of unemployment caused by economic changes: decline of old industries, depletion of
natural resources, movements of population, and adoption of labor-saving devices. In answer to other questions, he admitted that even if business were highly prosperous and steadily prosperous, there would be some men
out of jobs, because it takes time for them to shift from
one place to another, and from one industry to another.

The Professor evidently found these concessions helpful. 'I have felt all along,' he said, 'that your Policy cannot accomplish nearly as much as you seem to hope for.'

'We can't tell until we try,' answered the Business
Man. 'But suppose you are right. Suppose I *have* overstated the case. That is what an enthusiastic advocate
usually does — usually has to do in order to get a hearing,
as Plato or some other wise man observed many cen-
turies ago. Well, what does that matter? Suppose we

couldn't gain more than half what I hope for! Even so, isn't that enough to fire the imagination, enough to ——'

'Yes, more than enough,' the Professor broke in. 'Exactly how much you could achieve is not an essential point. Another point, however, which I have had in mind from the beginning, does seem to me important. I doubt if you can prove that business depressions are *initiated* by shortages of consumer income.'

'For my purposes I don't need to prove that,' the Business Man answered promptly. 'All I insist on, is that a decline of business, however initiated, cannot develop into a depression if consumer income is sufficiently sustained.'

'That is undoubtedly true,' said the Professor. 'But here is still another point. Is it not a mistake to try to sustain consumer income whenever the price-level begins to fall? Suppose the decline were caused chiefly by an exceptional circumstance, a bumper cotton crop, for example. Or suppose ——'

'You don't have to develop that point, Professor. I agree with you. As a business man, I know that a slight fall in the price-level may be helpful. It may result from large crops, or from temporary conditions in some one industry which, upon investigation, seem likely to correct themselves. All I urge is that such conditions be watched closely, to see whether corrective influences actually do get to work quickly enough.'

The Professor was evidently relieved to find himself so much nearer to agreement than he thought possible. 'That qualification,' he said, 'removes one of my chief difficulties. But turn now to an entirely different objection — this time a purely economic objection,' continued the Professor. 'If the new Policy succeeded, it would necessitate constant increases in the volume of money in circulation; but the time would come when no further increases would be possible, without abandoning either the gold standard or the present gold reserve ratio.'

'That is likely to happen whether or not the new Policy is adopted,' answered the Business Man. 'Some day, in order to provide enough money, we may have to adopt new measures for the purpose.'

'Just as we have done repeatedly in the past,' commented the Congressman 'The Professor seems like the little child in the story, constantly confronted by insuperable obstacles a quarter of an inch high.'

'As a matter of fact,' the Business Man continued, 'there is every reason to suppose that, after the new Policy has been in operation for a decade or two, and the entire country expects the continuance of prosperous times and a fairly stable price-level, we can safely provide for a larger volume of money by reducing the minimum gold reserve ratio. Then a lower ratio will serve just as well as the present ratio serves now. But, with our large gold reserves, we do not have to settle that question at this time. We shall be in a much better position to settle it, when the time comes, if we do what is needed now.'

'Yes, I suppose so,' admitted the Professor, his attitude plainly changing, as one objection after another was cleared away. 'And I now see that any one can endorse the new Policy, regardless of what his views may be concerning the Quantity Theory of Money. For every one knows that a sufficient increase in the volume of money spent by consumers stops a *decline* in the price-level of consumers' goods. And it is equally certain that a rapid *rise* in the price-level would be stopped, if a large enough part of consumer income, flowing into loans and taxes, did not flow back to consumers until a later period of time. That is not theory; it is arithmetic. In fact, the price-level of consumers' goods expresses little more than relation between units of money spent for goods and units of goods sold.'

'Go ahead, Professor,' urged the Gray Man.

'I can also see,' conceded the Professor, 'that for many years to come the construction of new capital facilities and public works at the right rate would more than make up the deficit of consumer buying due to savings, and thus give business all the stimulus it needs. But some people are sure to ask how business could get the needed stimulus after there were enough facilities to provide everything the people wanted.'

'Oh, come now,' the Gray Man protested, 'you can't seriously mean that any one would let that remote possibility prevent him from doing all possible good in *this* generation. We have to leave some problems for our great-great-grandchildren to solve.'

'No doubt,' said the Business Man, 'many other difficulties will be encountered in the future. We cannot settle them all now, or even foresee them. All we can hope to do now — all we need to do — is to agree upon the broad outlines of a policy. Real problems will remain: cultivation of higher tastes, as we have said, the problem of a more equitable distribution of wealth, the problem of capitalization of earning power and of land values. Real problems, these; but it will be easier to solve them after the flow of consumer income is rightly regulated. Whatever we do or do not do toward solving such problems, we must have the right flow of money.'

'Always leave something,' advised the Congressman, 'for the next session of Congress. No doubt, as Jefferson said, the next generation will be as wise as we are.'

The Business Man, who had been delighted all this while to have his plan turned over and over and examined on all sides, now said to the Professor: 'When I first outlined my Policy, you promised to offer several objections, and you have certainly kept your word. Have you any more to offer?'

'Not at present. At least, no objections to your theory. But I *do* object to calling it a system of economics. Important for practical purposes, I grant you; but at best, it is only a small part of economic theory. Certainly, it is not the core of the theory of land rent, for example, or of the theory of diminishing returns, or of the theory of marginal utility. A doctrine which has nothing to say about why some things are demanded and some are not; about why some industries succeed and others fail; about what determines particular prices as distinct from the general price-level — such a doctrine can hardly be called a complete system of economics.'

'That, of course, is true,' the Business Man replied. 'A conversation of this sort can hardly develop a complete system of anything. Moreover, I did not set out to develop a *system*. I set out to discuss the Gray Man's problem, and to find at least something that could be done about it. So I have considered only those aspects of economic theory which best served my purpose.'

'Leaving out many other aspects,' the Professor repeated.

'Granted. Still, I am convinced that John Stuart Mill was right when he said that any difference of opinion concerning his Automatic Consumption Theory involves radically different conceptions of political economy, especially in its practical aspects. To my mind, that is the same as saying that you can't deal effectively with the Gray Man's problem on the basis of the old economics. You must have something new — something fundamentally different. And so, Professor, even after all the concessions I have made, I still hold that some such theory as I have roughly framed — built around the central concept of the right flow of money to consumers — points to the most effective, immediately practical way of relieving want and anxiety.'

The Business Man paused and took out his cigar case. Then he leaned back against the cushion and shut his eyes. He was plainly tired; ready to call it a day's work.

But the Congressman was eager to press the discussion to a vote. 'Any further objections?' he asked.

'Not at present,' answered the Professor, 'but I should like to think the matter over.'

'What!' the Congressman exclaimed. 'You don't mean to say you have run out of objections!'

'Isn't it true,' asked the Gray Man, 'that all your doubts concerning the soundness and the practicability of the Policy have been cleared up?'

'Yes — but I might think of other objections.'

'You might, to be sure,' said the Business Man wearily. 'But without any effort, you can think of plenty of objections to doing *nothing* about it. You have spent your life studying these problems. All day we have been discussing them. I have introduced scarcely any facts which are not familiar to you. I have merely put the facts together in a new way, reaching a new conclusion; and you can see no fallacy in the reasoning. Moreover, you admit that for practical purposes I have sufficiently met all your objections. Is it reasonable for you to withhold your assent now, merely on the chance that some day you may think of other objections?'

'No, probably not. On economic grounds, your Proposal is soundly conceived. Possibly I might take exceptions to some minor phases; probably would; but that would not affect your main argument or your main conclusions. Every other programme which holds out as much hope is unsound; it would not work. But your Proposal, I repeat, is essentially sound.'

'Well, then, why not come out flatly in favor of it, and try to get a following among your fellow economists? Don't you think economists ought to give us all the hope there is, after having taught so much that is hopeless? Some of the most influential economists of the past century, as you well know, gave the people no grounds for expecting even as much progress as business men have actually made. Wouldn't it be a fine thing now for economists to join with business men in support of some such constructive, hope-giving policy as the one I have outlined?'

'It certainly would, and I may as well say now that I am convinced, and ready to do my part.'

'Congratulations, Professor!' exclaimed the Congressman. 'We now admit you to the goodly company of educated men.'

'Well, I may not deserve that honor,' said the Professor, doubtfully, 'but at least I have learned something to-day. To tell the truth, I now see a little good even in the old mercantilists. If orthodox economists had perceived what the mercantilists were groping for, but never reached, instead of seeing only their errors, there would have been less error in orthodox economics.'

The Professor paused. Again the Little Gray Man, his face beaming, urged the Professor to go on.

'Well, there is little more to say. The only reason I have held off so long is that my whole training keeps me forever balancing the two sides of every question, and unfits me for making decisions. But you are right. In this case, doing nothing is, in effect, making a decision against a policy which holds out immediate hope for progress.'

'So, at last,' said the Gray Man, his voice vibrant with eagerness, 'we are ready to consider what steps must be taken toward laying out the Road to Plenty.'

SECTION XV

IN WHICH THE ROAD TO PLENTY IS LAID OUT

'I HAVE never gone so far as to work out a definite programme, but now I am ready to do my part,' the Business Man declared.

'Don't know what my part is,' said the Semi-Silk Salesman, 'but, believe me, if all you want is the Sure-Fire Sales Shooters behind a plan to keep people buyin' — well, say, does a cat like fish?'

The Business Man proceeded: 'First of all, as must be clear from our discussion, the Plan should provide for finding the facts upon which action must be based. The most important facts are changes in the price-level of consumers' goods; that is to say, changes in retail prices.'

'For the reason,' explained the Professor, 'that such indexes show whether individual incomes are increasing at the right rate.'

'And so indicate,' said the Lawyer, 'when steps should be taken to prevent inflation or deflation. A rising index of prices means that demand is outrunning supply. Then the supply of goods must be increased or the flow of money to consumers retarded. A falling index, on the other hand, means that the supply of goods is outrunning the demand. Then the flow of consumer income should be increased. Is that what you mean?'

'In the main, yes,' the Business Man answered, 'but the procedure is not so simple as that. Other facts must be taken into account. Even when we have a far more dependable index of retail prices than has yet been made, we must still keep close watch of the factors which determine retail prices. Especially we must watch changes in consumer income, volume of production, volume of trade, foreign trade, and employment. Also, we must measure changes in the volume of money in circulation; the distribution of income among farmers, wage-earners, bondholders, and other groups; stocks on hand; projected expenditures of private concerns and of governments.'

'And also,' added the Congressman, 'changes in money rates, speculation, crop conditions, real estate prices and building construction.'

'Yes, they are all features of the moving picture that we must watch. What I want to emphasize is the fact that the whole picture must always be used as a guide to action, even though the trend of retail prices, in itself, will almost always show whether or not business is in a sound condition.'

'Still, it would be a mistake, as I think you intimated,' said the Lawyer, 'to try to stop falling prices, if the movement were caused by lower unit costs. In the automobile industry, for example, invention, mass production, and better management now enable one man to produce as much as three men formerly produced. That accounts largely for the lower prices of cars. If that were true of business in general, falling prices would be no cause for worry.'

'None at all,' agreed the Business Man. 'That shows what I mean by the necessity of taking the whole situation into account. If falling prices are accompanied by in-

creasing volume of trade, production, real wages, and employment — especially employment — there is nothing
to worry about.'

'There are still other conditions,' added the Professor,
'under which a slowly rising price-level may be exactly
what is needed. In any event, our own prices in the long
run must move in accord with world prices. But in general
you are right: the movement of domestic retail prices
shows, better than any other one index, whether anything
should be done toward increasing or decreasing consumer buying.'

'But I must say,' the Congressman admitted, 'that I
do not know much about index numbers. Are they always reliable?'

'Not always,' answered the Professor, 'because sometimes the statistics themselves are misleading. No index
number made from faulty data can be satisfactory. But
the best methods of constructing index numbers are sufficiently accurate for all practical purposes — the method
used by our Bureau of Labor Statistics, for example. The
instrumental error in such an index in any twelve-month
period seldom reaches one part in eight hundred.'

'One pound, more or less, in the weight of a horse: that
need not worry us,' observed the Congressman. 'There is,
then, no technical difficulty in measuring changes in the
data. The real difficulty, I suppose, is in obtaining satisfactory data.'

'That brings us to our next main question,' the Business
Man agreed. 'What agency is to collect the data? Some
national body, perhaps, such as the Chamber of Commerce of the United States. Once the importance of hav-

ing the information is understood, you can rely on business men to collect it. Our large corporations are already able to furnish a wealth of data — the Steel Corporation, for example, the General Electric Company, American Telephone, American Radiator, Sears Roebuck, to mention only a few. Some central agency could assemble the data.'

'But,' promptly objected the Congressman, 'you cannot expect the Government to depend on private help for the information on which it bases its own policies.'

'No, of course not.'

'Why duplicate the work?' asked the Gray Man.

'No need at all.' The Congressman felt sure about that. 'The Government,' he pointed out, 'is the only agency which represents all of us — consumers and producers, everybody; and it is the only agency which has authority to make everybody hand over the information.'

'You might add,' suggested the Professor, 'that the Government is better equipped than any other agency to give publicity to the data, once it is collected, and in a better position to furnish data which will be accepted as free from bias.'

'And you might add a reason which appeals strongly to me,' said the Gray Man. 'The purpose of collecting such data is the public good — the welfare of all of us. Why, then, should its use be confined to those who can pay private agencies for it? Why shouldn't the Government display storm signals for business men as freely as it does for mariners?'

'A good analogy,' the Semi-Silk Salesman cried with a wink at the Business Man. 'I'll say it for you.'

'So much for that, then,' said the Business Man. 'Now as I understand it, we have decided what data we need, how changes in the data are to be shown by means of index numbers, and what agency is to collect and issue the data. What next?'

'How about the cost of collecting the data?' asked the Lawyer.

'The cost will be small,' explained the Business Man; 'in fact, trifling, compared with the cost of business depressions, with their enforced idleness and wasted capital. No doubt, the depression of 1920 meant a total loss to the country of more than twenty billion dollars.'

'Then,' the Congressman declared, 'the ten-year cost would not be one per cent of the wealth lost in a single major depression. I never knew a business man who would not spend one dollar to forestall an almost certain loss of a hundred. Take my word, Congress will not balk at the expense of getting the information, once the Plan is understood.'

'As a matter of fact,' said the Business Man, 'the Government already collects much of the needed information, but uses it to little advantage.'

'I am glad you brought that in.' The Professor now spoke of what he knew from years of study. 'We hear a lot about waste of taxpayers' money, but few people have any idea of the masses of information which are now assembled by the Government and buried. Under our Plan, much of that information would be salvaged.'

'To the satisfaction of a great many of us.' The Lawyer evidently recalled some trying experiences. 'Business men do not now object so much to the trouble and expense of making out the elaborate reports which the Government demands, as to the fact that so little use seems to be made of those reports.'

'Having gathered the data, what is the Board going to do with them?' asked the Gray Man. 'Isn't that the next main question to be considered in any plan for action?'

'Naturally,' agreed the Business Man. 'And the first part of the answer comes straight out of our day's discussion. The Government, having adopted our Policy, must take all the assembled information into account in all its own fiscal decisions.'

'To save its own skin, if for no other reason,' commented the Congressman. 'Its own revenue depends on the prosperity of business. So you are right: for its own sake, the Government should make appropriations, borrow money, pay off loans, and pass other fiscal measures only after considering business conditions at the time and the consequent probable effect of the act in question.'

'In so doing,' the Business Man added, 'the Government will afford the necessary leadership to private business. At times, of course, the initiative of individuals will be sufficient; but at other times it will not. Private concerns may not dare to act alone; may not even be able to act alone. Relying on individual initiative is relying on chaos.'

'We don't depend on that to put out a fire or to win a war,' said the Salesman.

'No, we must have collective leadership,' the Lawyer declared. 'It can be furnished in part by private organizations.'

'But there are sure to be times when such leadership will not be enough.' The Business Man had been quick to see that the Congressman was right. 'That is necessarily so, because no private body has any responsibility for the general situation. Moreover, each must first look out for its own interests; but, as things are now, there are times when each can safeguard its own interests only by following policies which are bad for business in general. If, on the other hand, the Government itself acts under some such policy as we propose, that will change the whole situation so fundamentally that each private organization, still acting on its own initiative and for its own interests, will promote the interests of all.'

As the Semi-Silk Salesman was knitting his brows in perplexity over this point, the Business Man went on to say: 'You recall what was said this morning about the way in which every one, pursuing his own interests, does precisely what drives prices up, just as soon as he sees them well started up. If, however, every one knew that a powerful agency stood ready promptly to take steps which would check the upward movement, he would act accordingly.'

It was plain to everybody that the Government must provide the necessary leadership.

'But through what agency?' asked the Lawyer. 'That, I take it, is the next main issue.'

'I propose,' responded the Business Man, 'that the responsibility be fixed on a Federal Board, created for the purpose. But we must remember that precisely where the responsibility is located is not an essential part of our Policy.'

Whereupon the Lawyer promptly raised the objection that there are too many boards already. 'Why create another?' he asked. 'Why cannot the Federal Reserve Board carry out the Plan?'

'Because it has been created for an entirely different purpose,' answered the Business Man decisively. 'The Federal Reserve System, like all other monetary systems, is essentially a system for financing production. Admirable as it is for the purpose of providing sound money for responsible *producers* of goods, it has nothing to do directly with providing consumers with enough money to buy the goods. The Federal Reserve Board is performing its own work admirably, and that work will be just as necessary after our Policy is put into effect. By all means leave the Federal Reserve Board alone.'

'Clearly, then,' the Congressman concluded, 'to carry out our Policy, there should be a separate board.'

'Removed as far as possible from partisan influence,' said the Lawyer.

'Certainly; and if the new Board is even as satisfactory in that respect as the Federal Reserve Board, the success of the Plan is assured.'

'So far, so good,' said the Gray Man. 'What next?

'The next question concerns the functions of the new Board,' answered the Business Man. 'To my mind its first function should be to make reports of its findings concerning business conditions. In order to exercise its leadership effectively, the Board must make frequent, clear, public statements of its acts, its proposed acts, and the reasons therefor. The second function of the Board is to advise the Government. The Board should inform the President, Congress, and the various departments, from time to time, of the probable effect on economic welfare, in view of existing conditions, of taxes, tax rebates, refunding operations, payment of public debts, increase of wages and salaries, and other fiscal matters.'

'And in performing those two functions,' the Congressman added, 'it performs a third: it affords leadership to business.'

'That is the crux of the matter,' said the Business Man earnestly. 'Imagine what would happen if the United States Government announced its determination to use all its fiscal operations, as far as feasible, during the next twelve months, in order to achieve the purposes of our Plan. Just think of it! At once, business men everywhere would expect that business would be good — little danger of inflation or deflation; just an orderly market, keeping up with production. The result would be the most marked forging ahead of business that any country has ever known. I am willing to stake whatever reputation I may have as a business man on that statement.'

The Lawyer remarked that he knew several large concerns which would welcome such guidance. 'Often it is a toss-up,' he declared, 'in the minds of business executives, whether to build a new factory at once or wait a while; whether to order supplies for one month or for several months; whether to increase wage payments or continue on existing schedules; whether to produce for stock or only for current requirements; whether to declare extra dividends or accumulate larger surpluses.

When such options exist, it would be a real help to executives, if they could know which course the general situation calls for.'

'If they did know,' said the Business Man, 'they might act as wisely as the American Radiator Company has acted for many years. Basing its policy on the information which it has gathered for its own guidance, that Company has regularly bought large supplies of pig-iron when there were few buyers in the market. Thus it has helped producers to keep their furnaces in blast and their wage payments up at times when reduction of wages would have made a bad situation worse.'

The Congressman seemed to think that the action of a few such corporations, if taken before the sagging of prices had gone far, might well be enough to check the movement. In any event, he felt sure that where millions of dollars are involved, as in the case of the Steel Corporation and the Telephone Company, right decisions would be strong influences in the right direction.

'But it seems hardly enough,' said the Lawyer, doubtfully, 'for the Board merely to advise various departments of the probable effects of their acts.'

'Only experience can tell,' answered the Business Man. 'Possibly, at times it might not be enough. Consequently, some of the appropriations which Congress makes for public works should be expended over a series of years, the amounts expended in any given year to be determined by the Board, in accordance with the needs of the country as shown by current indexes. Under this arrangement, such amounts as were authorized by the Board would be expended by the proper departments.'

The Congressman was prompt and emphatic in his approval of this proposal. 'Under that Plan,' he explained, 'money could be put into circulation without any new machinery. The necessary amounts could be appropriated and expended, exactly as money is now appropriated and expended. That money could be — naturally would be — widely distributed, so that buying would be increased, when necessary, throughout the country.'

'Or the expenditures could be apportioned,' said the Professor, 'on the basis of known changes in the incomes of the States, so as partly to offset local business depressions due to crop failures or other temporary causes.'

'Such as the Mississippi flood,' suggested the Gray Man.

Then, in order to make sure how far they had gone, the Lawyer summed up what they had agreed upon. 'As I understand it,' he said, 'our Plan calls for a separate Federal Board, which shall itself gather and measure the data best adapted to show the adequacy of the flow of consumer income, using, however, for its own purposes, the wealth of data gathered by other agencies. Having thus collected the needed information, the Board shall advise the Government how to use it as a guide in all fiscal matters. The Board itself, guided in the same way, shall determine when certain expenditures are to be made, which already have been provided for by Congress, under a policy of long-range planning of public works. Thus the Board, both through its own acts and its published reason for its acts, will provide private business with the needed leadership. Does that cover the main points?'

'That sums it up, so far,' said the Congressman, now following every word with keen interest.

No need for the Little Gray Man to say how he felt: his face was radiant.

The Business Man proceeded with the Programme: 'The next point concerns the volume of money in circulation. If the indexes ever show the need of a reënforced consumer demand, which cannot be met without additional Government expenditures, the Board must have the power to bring about such expenditures out of funds previously accumulated for the purpose, or out of loans which involve an expansion of bank credit. This feature of the Plan is essential; because Government expenditures can do little to meet the needs, if all the money which the Government spends in a given period is collected as taxes in the same period.'

'It follows,' said the Lawyer, 'that the Government should borrow money to enable the Board to carry out its purpose whenever, in the judgment of the Board, the needed flow of money to consumers will not come from other sources. At most times, perhaps at all times, the needed expansion of money actually will come from other sources, because private industry will be stimulated, under our Policy, to make capital expenditures. And that is the chief way, as we agreed this afternoon, that consumers do obtain the needed flow of money when times are good. Still, we can never be sure whether the flow of income from this source will be too large or too small. The whole project is so very important that the Government should stand ready to borrow money if needed for the purpose.'

'Nothing new about that,' the Congressman declared.
'The Government now borrows money to cover immediate needs. Last spring, for example, following the usual
custom, the Treasury Department borrowed four hundred and fifty million dollars, through the sale of certificates of indebtedness, maturing next September and next
March. If necessary, money could be borrowed in the
same way to meet the needs of our Plan.'

'I get you,' said the Semi-Silk Salesman. 'When business begins to look rotten, more public spending. But
spending for what?'

'That is the least of our troubles,' answered the Congressman. 'Projects are already before Congress for
buildings, inland waterways, harbors, national highways,
and parks. Construction can be pushed forward or held
back, as the general business situation requires. Nothing
but the expense holds them back now. Nothing else kept
us from taking flood prevention measures in the Mississippi Valley long ago.'

'Such projects,' the Professor said confidently, 'would
put into circulation, as wages, all the money our Plan
could possibly require for decades to come. In that way,
we could sustain business and at the same time acquire
wealth. Public works built in that way might actually
cost the country nothing; for if they were not built, the
country might lose more than they cost, through the idleness of men and of capital savings.'

'How much better than handing out charity!' exclaimed the Gray Man. 'In order to accomplish our
purpose, it is not necessary to pay out money except for

services rendered. There is no need of making up deficits in consumer income by adding to pensions, or paying bonuses or doles.'

'Doles,' the Business Man declared, 'are a confession on the part of the Government of its failure to solve its most important economic problem.'

'The question is sure to arise,' suggested the Gray Man, 'to what extent it will be necessary under this Plan for the Government to make expenditures.'

'At present,' answered the Business Man, 'we have no means of knowing. Perhaps the need will be slight. We shall have to go slowly and find out. But don't forget that taking any step at all is a recognition of the nature of the problem and of the direction in which the solution is to be found. Just think what a great advance that will be over anything we have done in the past!'

The Lawyer then made a suggestion which every one saw was of the utmost importance. 'Business concerns,' he said, 'naturally want to grow. They do not curtail operations, as a rule, unless they fear a recession of business. So possibly the fact that they know that the Government stands ready to increase consumer income promptly, if the need arises, will induce them to increase their own capital expenditures at a sufficient rate to make additional Government expenditures unnecessary.'

'I think that will be the case most of the time,' said the Professor. 'So, also, when prices start to shoot upward, the very fact that the Government has declared its purpose of preventing extreme fluctuations will in itself help to achieve the purpose; for it will discourage speculation which thrives on shifting prices, and encourage enterprises which thrive on, and tend to preserve, stable prices. As we know from ample experience, if prices start up, it is in the interest of individuals to do the very things which drive prices farther up; whereas, under our Plan, it would be in the interest of individuals to do the very things which help to keep prices stable.'

'Certainly,' said the Business Man; 'and that brings us to the other side of the problem. Making up deficiencies in consumer income when necessary, and thus preventing a sustained *fall* in prices and in business, is only half the problem. The other half is preventing the rapid *rise* in prices and the unsound expansion of business which take place when demand outruns supply.'

The Lawyer was inclined to believe that the restraining influences of the Reserve System and warnings by various departments of the Government would usually be enough to curb a rapid rise in prices. 'If not,' he added, 'the new Board would not authorize additional expenditures for public works. Furthermore, it would oppose reduction in taxes, favor treasury surpluses, and take money out of circulation by borrowing it, and retaining it until business indexes show the need of putting it back. Of course, the Government can at any time and under any conditions borrow all the money it needs, merely by making the interest rates sufficiently high.'

'If desired,' suggested the Congressman, 'the required amount can be obtained directly from consumers, throughout the country, by selling bonds in small denominations, or even savings stamps through Postal Savings Banks.'

'In that way,' said the Business Man, 'inflation could be prevented. Now, I think we have roughly outlined all that is essential for carrying out my ideas. Many details, of course, will have to be worked out later. Don't you agree with me, Mr. Congressman, that we now have before us all that is necessary as a basis for action?'

'Yes, everything that we need now. How do you feel about it, Professor?'

'The Plan seems all right in general,' the Professor agreed, 'but exactly what would it call for in a concrete situation? Suppose we take some one period, say — well, for example ——'

'The year 1919?' the Lawyer suggested.

'Yes; the summer of that year.'

'Very well,' the Business Man replied. 'But bear in mind that such an inflated period is not a fair example; for under our Plan, unless I am wholly wrong, business would not have gone sky-rocketing in that way.'

'Sky-rocketing is the word!' exclaimed the Congressman. 'I remember how land prices in Kansas shot up; food prices, too.'

'And all other prices,' added the Lawyer. 'Throughout the three years prior to the summer of 1919, wages and the cost of living went up steadily and rapidly, and the general price-level rose over sixty per cent.'

'Even more significant for our purpose,' the Business Man remarked, 'is the fact that prices of the most sensitive commodities went up about thirty per cent in the first six months of the year, showing that we might expect further inflation during the next six months.'

'And yet,' said the Professor, 'volume of production was

actually falling off, and there was virtually no unemployment that could have been relieved by further inflation.'

'Clearly enough, then,' concluded the Business Man, 'further expansion of the volume of money would not bring increased production and higher standards of living, but merely still higher prices, more speculation in commodities, a dangerous approach to the minimum gold reserve ratio, and a collapse of business.'

'All of which economists pointed out at the time,' the Professor declared. 'And they were right. Twelve months more of inflation drove the cost of living up fully twenty per cent and wages still further; but there was no gain in production.'

'What the professors knew didn't help much,' said the Congressman, 'for there was no agency charged with the responsibility for knowing the facts, and invested with enough authority to take effective action. The question is, what would our Board have done at that time, in the light of the more comprehensive and more up-to-date information which our Plan calls for?'

In answer to that question, the Business Man again emphasized the fact that under the Proposed Policy, such a situation could not have developed. Furthermore, he pointed out, we cannot tell exactly what action the Policy would have required, because we do not know precisely what information under our Plan would have been available.

'In any event,' he added, 'the Board would have called public attention to the dangers. It would have published data to show precisely which branches of business were riding fastest to a fall. It would have opposed reduction in taxes and payment of public debts. At the same time, it would have authorized no further expenditures of the funds subject to its own control; and it would have shown the various departments of the Government why they should, as far as practicable, cease competing with private business for workers and materials. That, in itself, might have been enough to curb inflation.'

'And then?' asked the Lawyer.

'Then the Board would have watched the situation with the utmost care, in order to try to prevent a sharp reaction. Some reaction, no doubt, was inevitable. Nothing could have kept prices and general business activity at the level reached in the summer of 1919, since that level had been reached by means of inflation. But the Board could have done much to bring about a slow and orderly movement to a lower level.'

The Professor agreed. 'Still,' he objected, 'I should like a more definite idea of how the Board would function in a specific case. Your answer is not explicit enough to satisfy me.'

'Nor me, either,' replied the Business Man. 'I should like to pursue that question much further; but this is hardly the time to do it. Can you think of any other objections, Professor?'

'Yes, objections which we are certain to meet; but in the main, the Plan seems to be adequate. I strongly favor it. Still, you all know — too well, perhaps — how my mind works. I have to turn everything over and over, in an attempt to see all sides of it. This Plan of ours, for example, will be opposed by some people because they think it will permanently increase the public debt.'

'There is no reason whatever to think so,' said the Business Man. 'We cannot tell whether the chief need will be to increase or decrease the flow of money. Our Plan is just as likely to get the Government out of debt as to get it into further debt. Possibly increased tax receipts, due to sustained prosperity, will be sufficient to finance the plan. In the depression of 1921, Federal tax receipts fell off by a large amount. Don't you think, Mr. Congressman, that the Government could have saved itself that amount of revenue if, when prices first began to fall sharply, it had borrowed money and freely spent it on public works?'

The Congressman said he felt sure of that. 'Anyway,' he added, 'an increase of internal public debts is not necessarily a calamity. It means scarcely more than that the people of the United States collectively owe themselves more money. The country does not lose thereby.'

'On the contrary,' declared the Business Man, 'the country gains real wealth thereby — highways, canals, and the like — and in addition, all the real wealth which is produced by private industry, in excess of what would have been produced had business been allowed to suffer depression.'

'And the greatest waste of all is prevented, the waste of idle plants and idle workers,' the Gray Man said with feeling. 'Compared with that, what would it matter if Government debts were increased?'

'That is the point,' said the Lawyer. 'The question is, what the country has to show for its debts.'

'And the gains would be well distributed,' added the Gray Man. 'For wage-earners would receive larger shares of the national output. That is what happens whenever we are more prosperous than usual.'

'Note, in any event,' said the Business Man, 'that there is no ground for the assumption that our Plan would increase public debts. It may decrease both debts and taxes. It certainly would decrease the burden of taxation.'

'Still, you must admit,' said the Professor, 'that everybody takes it for granted that the country is doing well when it is paying off its debt. To such an achievement the party in power always "points with pride." '

'Yet, as a matter of fact,' the Business Man replied, 'there are times when a reduction of the public debt is not sound policy. All depends on the status of business. When production is far below capacity, and many workers are unemployed because demand for their products is insufficient, it is far better for the Government to spend money on public works than to use the money to pay debts.'

'That,' admitted the Congressman, 'is something I never thought of before. I can now see that every dollar which we used to reduce public debts in the depression of 1921 could have been used to better advantage in putting the unemployed to work.'

'Evidently, then,' said the Lawyer, 'the question really is when debts should be paid; how much now, how much later. Concerning that question, as I understand it, the new Board will make recommendations. It will also advise Congress concerning the best time and methods for incurring debts.'

'But' — the Gray Man was thinking of the reformers

he had met — 'some people will object to incurring public debts, even for our purpose, because they insist that the Government has the sole power to create money, and ought to create what it needs — never borrow and pay interest.'

'To that objection,' said the Business Man, 'we should make the same answer that we make to many other objections: We do not maintain that our Plan embodies everybody's pet reform. Charging interest on borrowed money may or may not be an evil. The present system of private banking may or may not be the best one. The point is that our Policy is necessary whether or not changes are made in these institutions.'

'We don't need to worry about such objections,' said the Lawyer, 'but there is one objection which the leaders of business may make. They may oppose our Policy because, at first sight, they may think it looks like further Government control of business.'

'We can meet that objection squarely,' affirmed the Business Man, 'by pointing out that under our Policy, as I said before, the Government interferes less with business than in the past. First, the Government provides more accurate and more comprehensive information than at present, and distributes it more promptly and more widely. That means less interference with business. Second, under our Policy, the Government administers its own expenditures with reference to the needs of business, slackening its competition with private concerns for men and materials when competition is keenest, and adding to the income of buyers when buying is falling off,

That also means less Government interference with business.'

'Don't forget,' said the Congressman, 'that nine tenths of the bankers at first opposed the Federal Reserve System itself. Too much Government interference with business, they said. Bunk! The Government now puts up storm signals at every port, without boarding the ships and telling the captains what to do. Can't the Government announce that it is a favorable time for expansion of plant, without taking control of the Steel Corporation? Our Plan leaves private business just as free as ever — doesn't exercise the slightest restraint on individual initiative.'

The Gray Man could see no grounds for that objection, anyway. 'The Proposed Policy,' he remarked, 'gives the Government no new powers. It merely provides for the more intelligent use of its present powers. As I understand it, the Government now has the sole power to levy Federal taxes, expend money for public works, regulate the currency, impose duties, and borrow money for Federal uses. In exercising these powers, the Government now affects business conditions, and will continue to do so. Inevitably. Even those who cry "less Government in business" do not propose to take these powers away from the Government. We are urging a plan whereby the Government, in using the powers it already has, will not only interfere less with business — which is merely an incidental advantage — but will increase human happiness everywhere. For my part, I can't see that the Government has any other excuse for being.'

'Still turning the Plan over, Professor? Discovered any new objections?' asked the Congressman.

'No well-founded objections; but the Plan is sure to be opposed on the ground that it will cause inflation. Some men cannot imagine the people having enough money without having too much.'

'That is absurd,' declared the Lawyer. 'Because governments have deliberately inflated their currencies by borrowing money or printing money to meet deficits, regardless of the effects on the price-level, is no reason why governments should not borrow money and use it for the avowed and deliberate purpose of preventing sharp price fluctuations.'

'Still,' the Business Man insisted, 'there will be plenty of people to condemn our Plan because they really think it means inflation. We shall have to stress the fact that the very gist and center point of the Plan is provision for a flow of money adjusted to the flow of goods; and that there is no other way to prevent inflation.'

'There is still another objection we shall have to meet,' said the Professor. 'Some people will argue that the United States cannot carry out such a policy unless other nations adopt it at the same time.'

'Sounds absurd to me,' cried the Semi-Silk Salesman.

'It is absurd,' agreed the Business Man. 'As a matter of fact, real incomes, volume of production, and volume of money on a gold basis, have for decades increased faster in the United States than in most countries, without interfering with foreign trade, or otherwise causing any trouble in international relations. This movement could go on even more rapidly, without causing trouble.'

'That is true,' assented the Professor. 'In any event, I feel sure that other nations would adopt similar measures. England especially needs them. And the more nations there are, the greater the advantage to the United States and to themselves, for they will have more buying capacity for our goods and larger markets for their own goods. Thus prospering, they will have no reason for resenting our prosperity. I don't see how we could better serve the world than by trying out this simple plan.'

That remark led the Congressman to speak again of the great advantage of so simple a proposal. To him it seemed much easier to understand than various other plans which are now in successful operation — the Income Tax laws, for example.

'Moreover,' said the Professor, 'it is not necessary for the people to understand the detailed mechanism of the Plan. It is enough for them to see whether, in general, the purpose is achieved. And that would be easy.'

'True,' assented the Lawyer. 'Just as any one, without understanding the intricacies of the Federal Reserve System, can see that we no longer have "money panics," so any one, without knowing the details of our Plan, could see that it was accomplishing its purpose. That is more than can be said for many other Government activities.'

'It certainly is a simple Plan,' said the Business Man; 'one which surely would have been put into effect long ago if false economic theories had not blocked the way.'

'Now, then,' the Gray Man exclaimed, jubilantly, 'we have all agreed on a Policy, and I don't see why everybody else should not agree on it.'

'Everybody but the extreme radicals,' said the Lawyer.
'It leaves them without a case.'

'The Red-Haired Orator would oppose the Plan; that's
a fact,' said the Gray Man. 'So would all the dynamiters.
But everybody else will surely be keen for it.'

Then the Congressman, turning to the Business Man
with the now familiar twinkle in his eyes, exclaimed,
'There you are, everybody convinced. And you are the
one who thought it was no use trying to have a serious discussion with dumb-bells like us. Now, will you apologize?'

'Gladly,' answered the Business Man, 'and at the same
time thank you all for a pleasant trip. Mighty good of
you to put up with so much talk.'

'Don't thank me,' answered the Professor. 'And
don't apologize. I am the one to do that.'

The Gray Man, stunned by the evident breaking-up
of the discussion, looked around for some one to protest
against ending everything in talk. But the Professor
went on: 'I now see that my remarks about the narrow
views of business men were too sweeping. You have
taken me out of my study, and given me a broader view
than I ever got from books, of what actually goes on in
business. You have shown a way — not the only way,
to be sure — but an exceedingly important way to make
progress. As a result, I now have a new groundwork
upon which to base much of my teaching; not wholly new,
I dare say, but at least this is the first time it has ever
been expounded so that I could get it.'

'I, too, have gained much from the day's discussion,'
said the Lawyer earnestly. 'The explanation of pro-

gress in terms of the flow of consumer income has cleared
up many points which have long puzzled me.'

'My case, exactly,' agreed the Congressman. 'I usually fight shy of debates, but I'm glad you brought me
into this one. Too bad to let the matter drop now.
Sorry so many flowers of speech can't bear a little fruit.'

'Talk was all to the good, I'll say,' added the Semi-
Silk Salesman. 'At least, what I could get through my
bean, and what I didn't sleep through. Just as well you
shut off my stories. Can't remember that story of the
blind beggar, anyway.'

'Well,' said the Business Man, 'many thanks to all of
you. And now it's nearly time for dinner; time, anyway,
that I slipped out and gave you a rest.'

'What!' exclaimed the Gray Man, in deep concern.
'You aren't — you can't mean ——'

But the Business Man, who was halfway to the door,
stopped only to say, 'Now, my Little Gray Man, you see
the way. Go to it!'

SECTION XVI

THE Little Gray Man slumped back into his seat, limp
with the sudden collapse of a great hope. He sat there
alone, holding his head in his hands, staring at the floor
and seeing nothing, not even noticing that all the others
had gone to dinner. Early in the day he had been elated
by the words of a man who knew — actually knew what
could be done in a large way, to lift unhappy men and
women above anxiety and want. Now it was clear that
the man who knew what to do had no intention of doing
anything. Slowly, step by step, that man had led him
over a steep trail to a mountain-top where, in all its
splendor, he had gained a glimpse of the promised land.
A glimpse — and nothing more.

Could it be true that the only way to that fair land was
the way of destruction? Was the Red-Haired Dynamiter
right, after all? Never — he had warned the workers —
never expect the capitalists and their hired men, the lawyers, to do anything for the workers — anything more
than hand out a little charity and a lot of advice.

That inflammatory appeal had left the Gray Man cold.
But now the sparks of the firebrand came back to him, as
he thought of that Business Man of knowledge and power
who, instead of himself plunging into action, had merely
said, 'Now, my Little Gray Man, you see the way. Go
to it!'

He laughed bitterly.

'A great chance I have,' he thought, 'of accomplishing anything. How far could I get with a programme like that? Unknown, without influence, without money, without power. Friends I have, to be sure, fine, loyal friends, but all equally helpless. One thing is certain: If Joe Burns depends on me for getting anything done, he has a forlorn hope.'

The thoughts of the dejected man went rushing back over a life of disappointments. As a boy, he had suffered from the breaking of his home and of his mother's heart, a tragedy which had found its beginning in the failure of his father to earn a living, a failure which had been caused, as the boy gradually came to see, by the progress of invention, which left his father skilled in nothing but an obsolete trade.

With all the passion and resolution of which a boy is capable, he had determined to give his life in some way — he had no idea how — to preventing tragedies like that.

Years later, in a severe depression of industry, he himself had become the center of a tragedy; and there had been little for him to do, day in and day out, except to think of all that such breakdowns of business mean in suffering. Yet, by a miracle, he had kept not only the ambition of his boyhood, but also the sweetness of his spirit.

As the years went by, time and again he had thought that at last the way had been found. Time and again he had been disappointed. Meanwhile, because he had won the confidence of men of large affairs, positions had opened up before him in the business world which promised incomes fabulous to him. They had tempted him, too; in his darkest hours, sorely tempted him. But always he had kept the courage of his Quest. Always he had hated the very word 'quitter.'

And now — now — in dejection, his youth and young manhood gone, he had to face the fact that he was still doing little more for the great cause than those men of large affairs, whose calling had seemed to him so sordid; little more than to distribute abundant advice and meager charity.

Through the dusty window, the Little Gray Man saw a line of trudging workers, stretching from the factory gates all the way down the ugly street. Another day's work done, he thought, and to-morrow there will be another, and the next day another. And beyond that, what? Endless anxiety, even for most of those who, by a special good fortune which they dare not hope for, actually do hold their jobs. How many of them, he wondered, if they had the choice to make to-night, would care to live over a day like the one now ending? How many of them, if they knew what the coming days had in store for them, would have the heart to go on?

Through the city the train flew; past row upon row of dreary factory dwellings; on and on into the country.

Down through a field, toward a dilapidated barn and a still more dilapidated house, came a farmer, leading a pair of horses. 'The plowman homeward plods his weary way,' thought the Gray Man.

Yes, and truly 'leaves the world to darkness and to me.'

For some time, clouds had been piling up in the west. Now, the Gray Man observed, the sky was as murky as the factory dwellings, as murky, almost, as his own spirit.

Soon the rain began to beat on the windows. He watched the drops as they gathered in little streams, wavered their way down the dirty panes, and were shaken off into space. Like himself — appearing suddenly out of the unknown, following for a moment an aimless course, buffeted hither and thither, and then, suddenly, off again into the unknown. What was it all about? What did it all matter? What did anything matter?

Useless, he thought, for me to allow myself to be crushed under the burdens of thousands upon thousands. The task is far beyond my poor powers. What I cannot help, I must forget.

So he stood up, summoned his old-time good cheer, threw back his head and shook himself, as if to cast off the burdens which bore him down. 'Yes,' he decided firmly, 'I will comfort myself at least a little, as others do, for they are right: I have set my life upon a hopeless Quest.'

But then, of a sudden, right before him appeared the eyes of Mary Marden, lustrous, perplexed, pleading eyes, just as that very morning they had followed him about the dingy chamber where she lay, with scarcely strength enough to turn her head.

At once, he knew that it was no use. He dropped back, limp, upon the seat. Thousands and thousands of sufferers, massed in a table of statistics — that he might forget. But one penniless, widowed mother, her new-born babe at her side, bereft, beseeching — that he could not forget.

Hard as he had tried to pull himself together, in the culmination of a life of disappointments, one frail human being, her eyes appealing straight to his heart, now overwhelmed him. His throat choking, his spirit quite, quite broken, he looked out across the wide meadows.

And it was more than rain that blurred the distant lights.

SECTION XVII

IN WHICH AN UNDERSTANDING WOMAN BECOMES
A COMRADE OF THE QUEST

TIRED and discouraged, the Gray Man sat alone in the smoking-room, reviewing the events of the day. Harder and harder he found it to keep his resentment from mounting toward that man of power and learning — that man who saw the light, but had no intention of following it. What right had such a man to say, 'It is not my job'? What right, until he had made every effort that lay within his power?

The Little Gray Man, his elbows resting on his knees, his fingers running through his rumpled hair, his eyes aimlessly following the pattern on the floor, was suddenly startled by a lurch of the train which all but hurled the Semi-Silk Salesman through the door and onto the seat in the corner.

'How's our Gray Man now?' asked the Salesman, as soon as he recovered his breath. 'Black, I'll say. Thought I'd find you in the dumps. Come, my boy, take a lesson from the Sure-Fire Sales Shooters. Don't be a quitter. Big business man? That's no reason for being afraid of him. Go after him again. You're just the one to land him.'

'I'm afraid not,' the Gray Man answered quickly; and almost as quickly, knew that he was wrong. He was taking precisely the attitude which he had just been condemning in another man. He himself had not done everything within his power; had actually been on the point of giving up the Quest.

True, he could not bring things to pass directly; but he might influence somebody who could. There on the same train was the Business Man, and there he would have to remain all the evening.

Now fully resolved, the Gray Man started for the drawing-room, stopping only to say to the Salesman, 'That was a sure-fire shot, if ever there was one.'

'You certainly may come in.' There was no doubt about the warmth of the Business Man's welcome. 'I am very glad you came. So is my wife.'

She smiled and gave him her hand.

Long afterward, when the Gray Man thought over that eventful journey, the part that shone forth like an evening star was the moment when that woman welcomed him, and as if by magic, the magic of her voice, perhaps, or her smile — he knew not what — dispelled all his diffidence, his fatigue, his discouragement. Now he *knew* that the Economics of Despair was only an illusion. For in that moment She (always afterward he thought of her as She), in that moment She had fully restored his faith.

As soon as they were seated, the Business Man said, 'My wife has been good enough to listen while I have given her a long account of our day's diversion.'

'From what I heard,' said She, 'I thought you were only a spirit, the spirit that gave life to the whole adventure. I am glad to find that you are more than that, for spirits have a way of vanishing into thin air, and your work is not done.'

'He it is,' the Business Man repeated warmly, 'who insisted on making the day enjoyable for me. Even the shots of the Sure-Fire Sales Shooter were close to the mark. Intelligent men, all of them. They helped me to clarify my own ideas. And to me the subject is fascinating.'

'I have come,' said the Gray Man, resolutely, 'to urge you to make it more fascinating by turning what you call a day's diversion into a life's passion.'

Thereupon the Gray Man threw himself into his plea with contagious enthusiasm. He was visibly encouraged — out of all reason, perhaps — by the presence of the Business Man's Wife. A depth of sympathy and understanding he felt in this serene, sensitive woman. She had done little more, it is true, than welcome him with a smile. And, as the conversation proceeded, She spoke only a few words, and those in a low voice. But they were eloquent. There was reason enough to take heart; for this woman of few words and quiet strength was plainly the dominant force in her husband's life. More than that, She had the courage of her emotions; and — blessings on Her — they were the Gray Man's own.

A Comrade of the Quest! And so, man of sense that he was, he became immoderately happy over moderate success.

The Gray Man felt, too, that he had another understanding ally in the 'goodly parson' who had just come in, the minister of the church attended by the Business Man and his wife. With them he was on his way to the Conference of Charities in Chicago. Friendliness and good-humor shone in his rosy face, a face at once boyish and mature. No wonder that children stopped him on the street, and strong men in trouble turned to him for sympathy, tolerance, and counsel. Soon the Gray Man found himself wondering whether he had known this gentle soul all his life, or whether that was merely the way everybody felt about him.

Hypocrisy, bigotry, false accusation, jealousy, stupidity; these and all the other discouragements that are the common lot of men of his calling, the Goodly Parson had met in the day's routine — met them as straws upon the tide of life — and he was still serene, radiant, confident.

Poverty he had known, as a matter of course, in his early life as pastor of an ordinary parish. And in the lives of his people, he had known nearly all there is to know of human frailty and sorrow, yearning and struggle. It had not occurred to him that his people needed to suffer — suffer. On the contrary, his deep concern was to help them bear the too-great suffering which, as yet, he had seen no means of preventing. So he listened understandingly as the Gray Man described the plight of the poor — the anxiety, the bewilderment, the despondency of men who are eager to work and can find no work to do — good men, whose children are stretching out their arms in vain.

The Gray Man told again in detail the story of Martin Barker; and again the Business Man was plainly moved.

'What I want to bring home to you,' the Gray Man added, 'is the fact that Martin's case is not a rare exception. Thousands of idle workers, with want nagging at them — victims of an industrial system they did not fashion and cannot fathom — are driven to desperation.

To what ends might you yourself not go, rather than see your loved ones hungry, at the very time when warehouses are bulging with food? I told you this morning what I should have done in Martin Barker's place; I should have stolen and gone to prison. In fact, that is precisely what I did do, for — I may as well tell you now — I am Martin Barker.'

'You!' exclaimed the Business Man, startled and dismayed. 'Then it was my father who sent you to prison. At the time of that depression, my father was President of the Carlow Company.'

'Yes, I know that; but I don't blame him. You are disturbed over the wrong thing; you miss the point. It was the economic structure which sent me to prison. And it was the economic structure which at the same time threw eight hundred Carlow employees out of work. Even as good a man as your father could not help it. He could not keep on, month after month, paying men to make goods which he could not sell. We all know that. He grieved as much as any one over the distress of the unemployed; and he gave generously of his own means for their relief, just as you are doing now. But when I look back on those hard times, and when I realize the full import of what you have said to-day, I cannot help thinking how paltry all your charity is and *must* be, compared with what you might do toward removing the *need* of charity.'

'It is just the thought I have had over and over again,' said the Pastor earnestly. 'Only the other day, down in the freight-yard end of town, when I looked in on that pitiful Rankin family, the one you went to see, I felt sure that most of such destitution might be pre-

vented. I wished that you, you with your grasp of the
sorry scheme of things that gave birth to such misery,
would get at the bottom of it all and show us a way out.'

'Sounds like collusion,' said the Business Man's Wife.
'That is what I told my husband last night, when we
looked over the Convention programme: "Poor relief,
unemployment doles, homes for aged couples, free mater-
nity beds." Must we go on the rest of our lives dealing
with nothing but "cases"? Can't we ever deal with
causes?'

She paused and regarded her husband. He would not
have remained silent so long, She felt sure, had he not
been deeply moved. She knew, too, that he was thinking
hard, and thinking to some purpose. She continued her
appeal: 'The more "cases" I look into at the Clark Street
Settlement, the more convinced I am that most of them
grow out of poverty which might have been prevented.
No doubt people who have acquired the habit of depend-
ing on us for help would be helpless now, under any industrial system; but they did not start life that way.
What ruined them was a combination of unemployment
and charity. I urged my husband last night to make
practical use of his theories; to show me what *I* could
do to help remove the causes of poverty.'

Social workers the country over, the Gray Man declared, have the same growing sense of futility. He, too,
was sure that most of the 'cases' with which he dealt
need never have become 'cases.' A single winter of excessive unemployment, he had found, creates more 'cases'
than all the charity boards in the country can take care
of. Always, he admitted, there will be plenty of work for

such organizations; always the need of friendly visitors like the Pastor; for there are causes of human distress which cannot be removed by the perfecting of mechanisms. But the *major* economic causes, he insisted, *can* be reached and *must* be reached.

'Meantime,' said She, 'most of the men who have brains enough to ferret out the deeper causes, and devise measures for removing them, do not make the attempt. Instead, they insist that not much can be done beyond handing out charity; that business is about as good as can be expected; that there is little real suffering, anyway; and that most of those who are without steady jobs have only themselves to blame.'

'No more than the usual amount of unemployment,' quoted the Gray Man.

'The main reason why the well-to-do believe all that,' She continued, 'is because they see no other way of gaining peace of mind. They have to believe it, in order to quiet their consciences and enjoy their wealth. And when, in spite of their sophistry, their consciences twinge a little more than usual, they give to charity a little more than usual.'

'To be fair to them,' suggested the Gray Man, 'we must add that they know nothing else they *can* do — wisely. They see that this radical programme and the other will do more harm than good — communism, single tax, abolition of private profit, and the rest; and they see no programme which they can support. So they do nothing.'

'No doubt,' She said, 'they are as eager as any one else to help; but in many cases their intelligence prevents them from enjoying the relief which some people get from indiscriminate charity and pursuit of futile reforms. You are right. Since nobody has ever shown them what they can do toward preventing poverty, I suppose they would be foolish to make themselves unhappy about it.'

'That's just it,' declared the Gray Man. 'I want such people to be shown the way; shown precisely what they can do, each and every one of them; so that they will no longer have any excuse for complacently accepting other people's suffering. Now you see why the bottom dropped out of everything when I was lifted to high hopes, only to find that no one had any intention of *doing* anything.'

'Don't imagine for a moment,' said the Business Man, now even more stirred than before, 'that I have been unmoved by your appeal. But bear in mind that I am a man of practical affairs, schooled to undertake nothing unless there is a good chance of putting it through.'

'How can you tell what chance there is without even trying?' asked the Gray Man. 'I feel sure that you could induce those men in the smoking-room to help put your Plan into effect. But you did not even suggest that they might *do* anything.'

'That doesn't sound like you,' said his wife. 'I can't imagine you taking the trouble to convince a board of directors what ought to be done, and then letting them adjourn without doing anything.'

'Not a perfect analogy, as you are well aware,' objected the Business Man. 'Business is business; and in business I am obliged to act. But reform is reform, and in that I am not obliged to act. Most reformers waste their time

and everybody else's; never get anywhere; a public nui-
sance. I have always thought I could do more good by
attending to my own business; and there are not enough
hours in the day for that. No Don Quixote crusade
against windmills for me!'

'But all I ask you to do,' insisted the Gray Man, 'is
what your own experience tells you is practical. There is
nothing visionary about your Policy. It accepts human
beings and human institutions for what they are. It involves doing little more than what we are now doing;
merely doing it all with a definite purpose, measuring
results, proceeding cautiously; in short, acting on what
any business man would call common sense. You don't
have to go tilting at windmills to lead such a movement.'

'But I have never thought of it as my job,' answered
the Business Man.

'Whose job is it, then?' asked the Gray Man. 'How
can you leave it to men like me? You would never think
of running a business that way. What chance have I of
bringing things to pass? I could talk to Joe Burns; I could
address the labor unions at Linton, I might even harangue the Red-Haired Orator's crowd in the public
square. What good would that do? Such people, unaided,
have no means of getting action. But pick out a hundred
leaders in politics and business, men whose decisions influence hundreds of others, men of the type you know
well, and the thing would be done. Isn't that so?'

'You know it is so,' said She. 'I have heard you say
that you could name twenty men who have influence
enough to bring any really good and feasible thing to pass;
men who would do it, too, if they made up their minds.'

'My own words, true enough,' admitted the Business Man. 'That is the way the Federal Reserve System was brought into being; and that step was more radical and more difficult for the people to understand than anything I propose. Yes, you are right; if a few men of sufficient influence could see what needs to be done, and all that it would mean in human happiness, those men could start a movement which would be sure to succeed. And, I must admit, a number of those men are among my intimate friends. I dare say I ought to urge them to do something.'

If the Gray Man was encouraged on first feeling the strength of her support, now he was elated. With even greater earnestness, he continued his appeal:

'Didn't you feel a thrill when that boy Lindbergh rose into the clouds alone, headed for Europe? And what were your emotions when you saw him welcomed by the heart of a nation? I can tell you. You felt like any other human being. For the moment, at least, you forgot that you were the sedate president of a corporation, a hard-headed director of the Federal Reserve Bank. Tears came. You tried to wink them away, not knowing whether to be proud or ashamed of them. Something had sounded depths in you which had not been plumbed since your own heroic youth. For the moment you had only one desire — to risk everything you had for some great end — to leap recklessly into an adventure that for *you* would mean nothing but sacrifice, but for humanity might mean *everything!*'

The Gray Man paused. Nobody spoke; but everybody knew what he meant, for everybody had felt just that way.

'The next morning,' continued the Gray Man, 'that

thrill was only a memory. Again you were nothing but a
very successful, highly respected, philanthropic, and up-
right citizen, with sound, well-diversified securities; a
practical man of affairs, with emotions fully controlled.
No danger *now* of doing anything your business associates
would look askance at; no danger of rising into the air and
flying alone after some intangible ideal.'

For a moment all were again silent; there was no sound
but the click-clack of the rails and the rumbling of the
train.

Then the Gray Man asked: 'After all, which man
would you prefer to be?'

'Ask him rather,' suggested his wife, 'which man he
really is, at heart.'

Then, turning to the Pastor, She said, 'Only last Sun-
day, you took for your text, "There was a man sent from
God whose name was John." And here is another, sent
to preach the Gospel in a Pullman car.'

'Our John,' the Pastor replied, 'might use for *his* text
the Iroquois Theater fire. When the building was in
flames and the people trapped, a care-free youth, happen-
ing along, stopped on the edge of the crowd to watch the
fire. Suddenly a frantic woman seized him by the arms.
"Good God!" she cried. "My children will burn to
death! Come with me and save them!" He did save
them, and then went back again and again, until he had
saved fifteen others. Afterward, when people praised him
for his heroism, he waved them aside, saying, "What else
could I do? The mother put it up to *me*."'

'And now we are putting it up to *you*,' She said, turning
to her husband with a look of unbounded confidence.

But it was plain that the Business Man scarcely heard these remarks; his thoughts were far, far away.

'I do not wonder,' She said gently, 'that you are thinking of the days of our youth. Our Servant in the House talks as you used to talk when I first knew you. How indignant you were, after that Chamber of Commerce meeting, at those comfortable leaders of business who said there was nothing they could do — that the unemployed had only themselves to blame. That night you were ready to brave the powers of darkness, single-handed. Then both you and I would have had contempt for a man who saw the way and refused to take the lead. When did we lose that spirit? Probably when we ourselves got comfortable.'

The Business Man sat looking at the distant lights, flashing here and there, through the gathering night. Presently his wife broke the silence.

'No one can ever make me believe,' She said, with a quiver in her voice, 'that that fine youth is any finer than my husband was when he was young.'

'You know,' She continued, 'how proud I am of all that you have since achieved. Still, I cannot help wondering whether we are not paying too high a price; whether it were not better to sacrifice success, if necessary — what our neighbors call success — and get back a passion for helping our fellow strugglers; helping them to avoid the *need* of our charity.'

He still stared through the cloudy window into the night, while his wife continued her appeal: 'After all, you would not be satisfied even if you attained your highest business ambitions, whatever they may be. The triumph

would be empty; you know that. Why not go back to the
fire and daring of your Lindbergh days? Shut your ears
to all the men around you who insist that everything
great is impossible. Hitch your wagon to a star. I cannot
find the star for you, but you have seen it. Why not follow
its light?'

All this while the Business Man had been deep in
thought, deep in yearning, too — yearning for the spirit
that gave zest to his youth.

'She is right,' he had been saying to himself. 'She is
always right. We grow old because we stop daring; we do
not stop daring because we grow old. Why should I put
off acting until the outcome seems certain; until I have
overcome every possible objection; until I have formu-
lated a Plan in its last detail? That is the professorial
attitude, not mine. I have never done business that way.
Nor have I ever waited until everybody agreed with me,
or held back for fear of what other men might think. I
may fail: that is true. But refusing to try — that would
be certain failure!'

Then he said aloud: 'The die is cast. Bring in the
others, my Little Gray Man, if you can induce them to
come — the Professor, the Congressman, the Lawyer,
even the Semi-Silk Salesman, if he is not exhausted.
Bring them all in, and together we will see what we can do
toward building the Road to Plenty.'

SECTION XVIII

IN WHICH A START IS MADE ON THE ROAD TO PLENTY

'WHAT can we do about it, and do right away?'

The Business Man spoke earnestly. Everybody in the crowded drawing-room saw that he was now as eager for action as the Thorn in the Flesh had been from the outset. He went on, speaking rapidly and decisively: 'I had not thought of doing anything, myself, toward putting the Plan into effect. But our Gray Man is right: everybody ought to do what he can toward bringing action.'

'Action is the word,' echoed the Congressman. 'Count on me.'

'And on me!' cried the Semi-Silk Salesman, with animation. 'Sure-Fire Sales Shooters, not much on theory; but give 'em somethin' to shoot at, an' they don't use no blank cartridges!'

'We are all ready to help,' the Lawyer declared. 'The Professor tells me that certain researches, which he will get under way at once, ought to give us a more convincing statistical basis. That may help.'

Thus encouraged, the Business Man proceeded: 'For my own part, I shall do everything I can to arouse discussion; but first of all I shall take a firm position, publicly.'

'Good!' said the Lawyer with conviction. 'Nothing can help more than for men of your standing to come out openly and flatly in favor of the Plan.'

'Anyway,' the Congressman remarked, 'it is men like you who will have to show us what has to be done. Sena-

tor Jones hit the nail on the head the other night before
the Academy of Political Science. He insisted that men
who are intimately acquainted with business are best
fitted to devise means of keeping business prosperous.
The Senator hopes that a committee of such men will
furnish Congress with a concrete plan.'

The Business Man called attention to the fact that a
committee of one hundred men of affairs had already been
organized for the purpose of advising the Government on
business needs. 'I will bring our Plan before this committee,' he said; 'and if it does not choose to act, I will find a
committee which *will* act.'

The Congressman said that he needed the help of some
such committee in drawing up a bill. 'But don't be disturbed,' he added, 'if the bill is pulled to pieces, amended,
and only slowly whipped into shape. Good laws are born
full-grown about as often as men are.'

'That doesn't matter,' said the Business Man. 'Remember that we are not insisting on details. Any bill will
do which embodies the right principles.'

The Lawyer felt sure that several departments of the
Government were prepared to support such a bill. He
spoke of measures, already adopted by the Treasury Department and the Federal Reserve Board, and new activities of the Department of Commerce, which are fully
in accord with the new Policy.

'Notably so,' the Congressman declared. 'As a matter
of fact, every department can further its own policies by
furthering ours. So can everybody else, for that matter:
labor and capital; farmers and manufacturers; all sections
of the country, North, East, South, West — everybody.

All political parties, too. No party is committed to anything inconsistent with our purpose.'

'Wage-earners will be with us, anyway.' The Gray
Man felt sure of that. 'The American Federation of Labor has long insisted that wages should increase as rapidly
as production. Now we have a feasible plan for bringing
that about. And this is where *I* come in. I am leaving
you at the next station, to spend the night with one of the
officers of the Federation. I'll get *his* support; and it
won't take all night, either.'

'Don't stop there,' urged the Congressman. 'Get *all*
labor organizations to study the Plan. And I'll get the
engineers. Take my word, they'll be quick to grasp the
idea. The American Federated Engineering Societies are
now supporting the Wynant Bill. That provides, you
know, for coördination of various Government functions
under a Department of Public Works and Domain; calls
for systematic development of public works with due reference to the needs of business. The idea is sound, of
course; but it can't be carried far until the Government
adopts some such policy as we propose. Yes, you can
count on me to get the Plan before the engineers.'

'And you can count on Secretary Hoover to urge them
to support it,' added the Business Man, 'judging from the
sound remarks he has made on the subject.'

The Lawyer, on his part, agreed to get in touch with
the people who are seeking a means of stabilizing the purchasing power of money. 'Our Plan,' he pointed out, 'is
the only workable means of doing that, which provides
constant incentives to increased output. All the other
plans I know anything about ignore the fact that we can-

not stabilize the dollar merely by controlling the *gross* volume of money in circulation, regardless of the amount spent for consumers' goods.'

The Professor agreed. 'For that reason,' he said, 'we ought to gain the support of many people who are convinced that stable money is a paramount need, but who have not yet heard of any feasible means of accomplishing the purpose.'

The Congressman promised to have the Plan considered by various other private organizations, including chambers of commerce, trade associations, and farm groups. But the press, he felt sure, could be of even greater help. 'Do all you can to interest the editors,' he urged. 'They will stir up discussion everywhere, once they see the new light which all this throws on many public issues which they have to write about every day.'

'Women's clubs ought to be informed, too,' added the Business Man's Wife. 'Many a club which has felt the urge to do something will now find something feasible to do.'

'And don't forget us. First man on the band-wagon will be the guy who has to sell goods.' No need for the Salesman to argue that point; they all knew that he was right.

'There's one obvious thing for *me* to do at once,' the Professor remarked thoughtfully; 'embody the essentials of our scheme in my address at Chicago, on the economics of unemployment. Social workers there and everywhere else will be with us.'

'The churches, too,' said the Pastor. 'I'll get some of them to help. Talk about business without a buyer! The problem of the churches is religion without a buyer; partly because they, too, have always preached a Dismal Science — "Abandon hope of worldly goods, all ye who enter here!"'

'Lucky business men didn't abandon hope!' the Congressman exclaimed. 'Where would we be now, if they had set their minds on the life beyond, and given up the struggle for wealth! We must give the ministers a new hope; give them ——'

'Give them,' broke in the Business Man, 'grounds for saying to the poor, what the best of them have always wanted to say: "No sense in being resigned; there *is* a way out."'

'And saying to the rich,' added his wife, '"You have no right to comfort yourselves with the thought that you can't do much of anything about it."'

'That's it,' agreed the Pastor. 'Now we have a Plan which all denominations can support — Christian, if anything ever was, for the good of everybody, especially the most needy.'

'Too bad the Bishop couldn't hear that!' murmured the Gray Man.

'Never mind him or the other Wise Men of the East,' said the Lawyer, disdainfully. 'Such men take their ideas from other people. They'll fall in line as soon as they find it is the thing to do.'

The Business Man then urged everybody, when explaining the Policy, to be sure to emphasize the fact that it requires us to do little more than we are now doing; merely doing it all with a new purpose and new guidance; taking people as they are; not speculating on what might

be done, if men and women did not act like human beings.

'Since they *do* act like human beings,' warned the Congressman, 'we mustn't be discouraged if we can't get
everything done in a day. Let's go as far as we can go.'

'And don't be disconcerted,' added the Business Man,
'if you hear objections which we haven't had time to discuss to-day. Write to me about them, whenever you
think I can help you out. Meantime, I'll draw up a plan
of procedure, and send it to each of you for criticism. Let
me have your addresses before we break up.'

'Take mine now,' said the Gray Man, as the train began to slow down. 'This is where I must leave you.'

As radiant at that moment as he had been dejected a
little while before, the Gray Man said good-bye to the
group — friends all, for they had written him down as
one who loves his fellow men.

'Comrades of the Quest,' he said, with a tremor in his
voice. 'My hopes are in your keeping.'

At a turn of the road, just above the railroad station,
the Gray Man watched the train as it rushed on through
the valley; on and on, the brilliant headlight piercing the
gloom, a symbol — so it seemed to him — of the light of
learning, revealing the Road to Plenty. Many times
before, as he had watched the long and mystic line, of
lights of a departing train, winding its way into the
night, he had felt a thrill.

But never such a thrill as now.